The Phenomenal Power of Thought

The Phenomenal Power of Thought

Originally Published as *Thought-Force in Business and Life*

William Walker Atkinson

STONEWELL PRESS

ISBN 978-1-62730-070-4

Published by Stonewell Press, Salt Lake City, Utah.

www.stonewellpress.com
editor@stonewellpress.com

CONTENTS

Publisher's Preface

This classic little book, first published in 1900, uses occasional terminology that may be unfamiliar or seem outdated. And some of Atkinson's ideas are clearly speculative. Nevertheless, this book is offered with the confidence that much of the content will be of value to the twenty-first century reader.

Some of Atkinson's other works include *The Secret of Success* and *The Power of Concentration*.

Author's Preface

In justice to myself, I think it well to state that this work has been somewhat hastily prepared from the notes used by me in certain of lectures, the lessons give herein practically being the syllabi of the said lectures. In the lectures, and in this work, my one and only purpose has been to acquaint the students with the means of developing, and effectively using the might forces latent within him—Personal Magnetism and Psychic Influence. To this end I have scarified all pretensions to literary style, all attempts to secure felicity of diction. I have felt that I had a message to deliver, and I endeavored to deliver it promptly, clearly and plainly, without any attempt at "fine writing." If a homely word seemed to express my thought—I used it. If a slang term or semi-slang phrase seemed to fit in—in it went.

I trust that my critics will spare themselves the trouble of pointing out my many defects of style and composition—I fully realize these things. I have subordinated everything else, in my endeavor to make this work plain and practical. This is an explanation, not an apology.

With the above understanding between us, I submit this little work to your kind consideration. Whilst fully cognizant of its defects, I still feel that it will be helpful to some of the many who are endeavoring to overcome unfavorable environments, which it may serve as a guidepost, pointing out the past to better things. I feel that it will do its share of the work of removing Fear thought from the minds of men, of replacing "I Can't" with "I Can and *I Will*." I feel that I must do these things, for it contains within it the germs of a mighty Truth.

William Walker Atkinson
Chicago, Illinois,
December 1900

Chapter 1

SALUTATORY

Views of other writers—Erroneous theories—Vegetarianism—Celibacy—Vital Fluid—
Deep Breathing—Real progress made by investigation, not by theories—Existence of
personal magnetism unquestioned—A self-evident truth—Results, not theories—No pet
theories advanced—Accept nothing that you cannot demonstrate.

The nearer to the practical men keep
The less they deal in vague and abstract things
The less they deal in huge, mysterious words
The mightier is their power.

(Thomas L. Harris)

"Theories are but mighty soap-bubbles, with which the grown-up children of science amuse themselves." The majority of writers upon this subject have devoted nearly all their efforts, as well as their space, to proving, first, that Personal Magnetism really existed; and, secondly, that the phenomenon was best accounted for by some pet theory of their own. Some attribute the power of influencing men to the use of a vegetarian diet, notwithstanding the fact that some of the most "magnetic" individuals "make graveyards of their stomachs." Others insist that in celibacy and abstinence from sexual intercourse may be found the secret, notwithstanding the fact that the majority of "magnetic" individuals do not differ in their sexual customs from their less magnetic brothers. Others hold that the "magnetic" force abounds in the air around us to absorb great quantities of the vital fluid, charging ourselves with force in the manner of the storage battery. And so on, each with his little pet theory.

Now, I have no fault to find with the systems above mentioned. Although not leading a life of celibacy, I see much good in the doctrine of continence, and there can be no two opinions as to the merits of chastity; whilst not accepting the theory of the absorption of "magnetic force" from the earth's atmosphere, I am a firm advocate of, and believer in, "deep breathing, " and believe that if the same was universally practiced much sickness and physical weakness would disappear from the earth. All these things are good, but a little reflection will show anyone that they are not the prime factors in the production of the quality known as "Personal Magnetism." The writers on the subject usually conclude by telling their readers of the wonderful possibilities open to anyone who can acquire this power and learn how to use it. They, however, say little or nothing of how this force may be acquired, that is beyond stating their theories. They deliver discourses—but do not instruct.

They are preachers—not teachers. They dwell upon theories—and neglect facts.

The real progress in this branch of scientific research has been made, not by writers or theorists, but by a few earnest investigators who have conducted numberless experiments, and have explored every avenue of information, and who have brought this wonderful subject out of the realms of mere speculation and placed it upon a scientific basis.

The writer has been a close student and investigator of this subject for many years, and the present work is an attempt to give to his students some of the fundamental principles derived from the investigations and practical experiments of himself and his co-workers in this field. Our lessons, therefore, will be confined, so far as is possible, to statements of proven facts, and practical instruction, touching upon theory only when absolutely necessary.

In my opinion, I would insult your intelligence if I were to present to you an elaborate argument, the purpose of which would be an attempt to prove the existence of that wonderful force, latent in man, developed by the few, but possible of acquirement by all; that mysterious quality called, for want of a better name—Personal Magnetism.

To set out to prove its existence, would be akin to an attempt to convince the average intelligent man of the fact that the magnet influences the needle; that the X-rays penetrate the body of man or still more solid object; that a message be conveyed by electricity, along a beam of light, or even by wireless telegraphy, through the air without the need of any other medium. Every intelligent person is aware of the existence of the above-mentioned phenomena, and does not need to have the same demonstrated to him. If he is interested in the subject at all, he wishes to be taught how to permeate these forces, so that he may be able to reproduce the experiments himself. This is equally true of the student of Personal Magnetism. He has long since learned that such a force exists. He sees it around him everyday, and knows of the wonders that are accomplished by its aid. He, possibly, is aware that he has developed the force to a certain degree, and what he wants, in any event, is to become acquainted with the means whereby he can fully develop and intelligently use the force latent within him. I therefore shall make no attempt to demonstrate the existence of the force, believing it to be self-evident.

I also intend to avoid a tiresome discussion of the numerous theories, which have been advanced to account for the phenomenon of Personal Magnetism. I have no pet theory to advance. I will endeavor to teach you how to obtain results, and you can then read up on the subject of theories, or possibly formulate a new theory of your own. I will state briefly my own conception of the cause underlying the phenomena alluded to in this work, but I shall not attempt to force my views upon you. You are at liberty to accept or reject any theory, as the result in no way depends upon any special form of belief. Many of those who have obtained the best results, have discarded one theory after another, and now say that they do not attempt to explain the real cause underlying the results, being content to work on, without a dogmatic theory, so long as they know how to obtain the results. With this explanation, I will leave the land of theory and enter into the realm of practice, and will endeavor to so instruct you along the lines of the development and use of this mighty force, that you may reproduce the results already obtained by others, and perhaps may become investigators and leaders in the work of blazing the way through the woods of superstition and mystery with which the subject has been surrounded so long. I will ask you to accept nothing that you cannot prove.

Chapter 2

THE NATURE OF THE FORCE

The force not magnetic in its nature—Subtle current of thought waves—Thoughts are things—Our thoughts affect ourselves as well as others—Change of appearance following change of occupation—Thought the greatest force in the world—"I can and I will" vs. "I can't"—Practical instruction not transcendental discourse—The adductive power of thought—Fear thought the root of injurious thinking.

To the minds of most people, the term Personal Magnetism conveys the idea of a current radiating from the person of the magnetic individual, drawing to him all those within the radius of his magnetic force. This idea, whilst on the whole erroneous, still contains within it the germ of the real truth. There is a current of attracting force radiating from man, but it is not a magnetic force in so far as the term "magnetism" implies some connection with the lodestone or electricity. The human magnetic current, whilst bearing some resemblance to these two familiar forces in its effects, has no real connection with them so far as is concerned its origin or intrinsic nature.

That which we call Personal Magnetism is the subtle current of thought-waves, or thought-vibrations, projected from the human mind. Every thought created by our minds is a force of greater or lesser intensity, varying in strength according to the impetus imparted to it at the time of its creation. When we think, we send from us a subtle current, which tables along like a ray often far removed from us by space, a forceful thought will go on its errand charged with a mighty power, and will often bear down the instinctive resistance of the minds of others to outside impressions, whilst a weak thought will be unable to obtain an entrance Trance to the mental castle of another, unless that castle be but poorly guarded. Repeated thoughts along the same lines sent one after the other, will—often effect—an entrance where a single thought-wave, although much stronger, will be repulsed. It is an exhibition of a physical law in the Psychical world, and exemplifies the old saying about steady dripping wearing away a stone.

We are all influenced much more than we are aware by the thoughts of others. I do not mean by their opinions but by their thoughts. A great writer on this subject very truly says: "thoughts are things." They are things, and most powerful things at that. Unless we understand this fact, we are at the mercy of a mighty force, of whose nature we know nothing, and whose very existence many of us deny. On the other hand, if we understand the nature and laws governing this wonderful force, we can master it and render it our instrument and assistant. Every thought created by us, weak or strong, good or bad, healthy or unhealthy, sends out its vibratory waves, which affect, to a greater or lesser extent all with whom we come in contact, or who may come within the radius of our thought vibrations. Thought waves are like the ripples on a pond caused by the casting in of a pebble, they move in constantly widening circles, radiating from a central point. Of course, if an impulse projects the thought waves forcibly toward a certain object, its force will be felt more strongly at that point.

Besides affecting others, our thoughts affect us, not only temporarily, but also permanently. We are what we think ourselves into being. The biblical statement that "as a man thinketh in his heart, so is he," is literally correct. We are all creatures of our own mental creating. You know how easy it is to think yourself into a "blue" state of mind, or the reverse, but you do not realized that repeated thought upon a certain line will manifest itself not only in character (which it certainly does), but also in the physical appearance of the thinker. This is a demonstrable fact, and you have but to look around you to realize it. You have noticed how a man's occupation shows itself in his appearance and general character. What do you suppose occasions this phenomenon? Nothing more or less than that thought. If you've have changed your occupation, your general character and appearance kept pace with your changed habits of thought. Your new occupation brought out a new train of thought, and "Thoughts take form in Action." You may have never taken this view of the matter, but it is true nevertheless, and you may find ample proof of its correctness by merely looking around you.

A man who thinks Energy manifests Energy. The man, who thinks Courage manifests courage. The man who thinks, "I can and I will," "gets there," while the "I can't" man "gets left." You know that to be true. Now, what causes the difference? Thought—just plain thought. But why?—Just because it cannot help itself. Action follows as the natural result of vigorous thinking. You think in earnest, and action does the rest. Thought is the greatest thing in the world. If you do not know it now, you will before you are through with this course of lessons. You may say that this is no new thing to you—that you know all about "making up your mind," and all that sort of thing, long ago. Then why did you not put it into practice and make something of yourself? I will tell you the trouble. You thought "I Can't" instead of "I Can." Now, I am going to change that "I Can't" into a big "I Can" and a bigger "I Will." That is what I am here for, and I intend to "make you over," before I am through with you. I suppose that you thought I would give you an elaborate, transcendental discourse on things away up in the clouds, and hoped that I would tell you how to charge yourself up with a lot of magnetism, so that you would be able to light the gas with the tips of your fingers, or draw everybody to you like a piece of steel to a magnet, now, didn't you? Well, I am not. But I intend to tell you how you can generate in yourself a force, compared with which magnetism is weak; a force that will make a man of you; a force that will make you realize the I AM within you; a power that will enable you to be a man of strong personal qualities; a man of influence; a successful man. I will tell you how you can acquire that which you have been calling Personal Magnetism, providing you will start at it in earnest. It is worth working for, and when you feel your new strength developing within you, you would not exchange your newfound knowledge for a fortune.

Why you feel a little stronger already, I don't you? Of course you do. I never have talked five minutes to a class of students as you do. I never have talked five minutes to a class of students about "I Can and I Will" and about the I AM within them without their throwing back their shoulders, raising their heads, taking a long breath, and looking me square in the eyes as a man or woman should. It was "thought manifesting itself in action." Do you see the point? I had planted the little seed of self-knowledge, and it had begun to sprout.

Before I conclude this lesson, I wish to direct your attention to one other very important thing about thought, and that is the Adductive Power of Thought. Pay attention to this; please as it is of the highest importance. Avoiding all attempts at a scientific explanation, and keeping away from technical terms, I will state the matter concisely thus: Thoughts attract like thoughts; the good thought attracts other good thoughts; the bad thought, the bad; thought of strength, likewise; thoughts of discouragement and doubt follow the rule, and so on through the entire gamut of thoughts.

Your thought attracts to it the corresponding thought of others and increases your stock of that particular kind of thought. Do you see the point? Think Fear thoughts, and you draw to yourself all the Fear thought in that neighborhood. The harder you think it, the greater supply of undesirable thought flocks to you. Think "I am Fearless," and all the courageous thought force within your radius will move towards you, and will aid you. Try it. That is, try the latter. Don't think Fear thought.

Fear and Hate are the parents of all the vile thoughts. I will go into this matter with you at greater length in subsequent lessons, but let me urge upon you now, with all the earnestness of which I am capable, to tear out those wile seeds—Fear and Hate. Tear them out by the roots. They spoil the whole garden and breed a host of other weeds, such as Worry, Doubt, Timidity, Lack of Self Respect, Jealousy, Spite, Malice, Envy, Slander and Morbid Ideas. I am not trying to preach you a sermon, but I know that these vile thoughts are hindering your progress, and you will realize it, too, if you will stop to thinking for a moment. Open the blinds, and let the pure sunshine of Bright, Cheerful and Happy thoughts pour in, and the microbes of Doubt and Despair and Failure will leave, and seek more congenial quarters.

If you were my dearest friend, and I knew that this message would be my last on earth, I would shout to you, as loud as my vocal organs would permit: *"Let go of fear and hate thoughts."*

Chapter 3

HOW THE THOUGHT FORCE CAN AID YOU

Success dependent upon Personal Influence—"Strong men arrive"—Apparent exceptions to the rule—When negative men produce; positive men reap the benefit—Money the material manifestation of success—Money a means, not an end—The Law of Mental Control—Influence through suggestion—Influence by thought vibrations—Influence by thoughts adductive power—Influence acquired by character building.

I am addressing you upon the supposition that you are desirous of developing the forces within you, for the purpose of attaining success. Success in life depends very materially upon the possession of the quality of attracting and influencing our fellow men. No matter what other qualities you may possess, you are handicapped by a lack of that subtle force which we are in the habit of calling Personal Magnetism. Look around you and you will see that nearly every man who has "arrived " is possessed of the ability to attract, persuade, influence or control his fellows. They are all what is known as "strong" men. There are a few exceptions to this great rule, and these exceptions only go to prove the rule itself. These exceptions are usually found among men who have demonstrated their success along the lines of art, scientific research, invention, literary work, etc., and it will readily be seen that their success, from the very nature of things, depends more upon a close, concentrated, plodding research or effort, rather than upon push, energy, force and knowledge of human nature, or ability to handle men. These men are successful in their own lines of endeavor, but, as a rule, the results of their labor are reaped by others of more worldly turn of mind. If these burners of midnight oil meet with financial success, it is because some more positive man has taken charge of the business end of their work and pushed it through, in which case the said positive man usually reaps the lion's share.

This being the true state of affairs, I am justified in regarding success as meaning the attaining of financial reward, and that must depend largely upon the Personal Magnetism of the seeker of success. The inventor, student, writer, and scientist can be greatly benefited by an understanding of the intelligent use of the powers of Mental Control, but to the "man among men" remains the privilege of securing the best results of that wonderful power, for it brings him not only Success, but also its material manifestations—Money.

Money, regarded as mere money, is not a high ideal, but regarded, as the means of surrounding ourselves with the best things of like, it becomes no unworthy goal for human endeavor. I, therefore, feel, justified in treating it as the end to be sought after.

To repeat, success in life depends largely upon our ability to interest, attract, influence and control our fellow men. I do not think that you will require any argument upon that point, that is if you have had any acquaintance, whatever, with the world of men and affairs.

The next thing is to learn how this wonderful and valuable power may be acquired. The answer is: by the mastery of the law of Mental Control. That is the secret of not only Personal Magnetism, but also of Success in Life and of Happiness as well. To the man or woman who masters this law, the world is an oyster to be opened and enjoyed in comfort. Even he, who lacks the application and perseverance to follow up the exercises for the development of his latent power, will be stronger and more positive from a mere acquaintance with the subject. "This is all very well," you say, "but tell us how we may develop this power." That is just what I am doing now. I am leading you up to an understanding of the theory, by easy steps. I wish the idea to unfold naturally, so as to avoid giving you mental dyspepsia.

Now, for a summing up of the general theory, before I take up the subject in detail.

I have told you that the power of thought could be used in a number of ways in the direction of influencing men and gaining success. I have given you an idea of how thought operates in the direction named. Before proceeding to our next lesson, I think it well to again call your attention to the several different ways in which thought can aid you in attaining success, through the influencing of men.

Thought will aid you in the following manner:

1. By the use of your positive thought force in the direction of directly influencing men in person, through the law of Suggestion. By this I mean that you will be able to interest men in your schemes and plans, enlist their aid, secure their patronage, and influence them generally. This faculty, natural to some men, can be acquired by any man or woman who has the will power and perseverance to develop it within them. Most students of the subject are desirous of acquiring knowledge of this branch of Mental Control before the other phases of the subject, and I, therefore, will take it up in my next lesson.

2. By the power of direct thought vibrations set in motion by your mind, which will exert a powerful effect upon the minds of others, unless they understand the secret of guarding against these forces and rendering themselves positive to others. An understanding of this law will also enable you to present a positive mental attitude toward the thought waves emanating from the minds of others.

3. By the power of the adductive qualities of thought, which works upon the theory "like attracts like." By holding certain thoughts constantly, in your mind, you attract to you thoughts and influences of the like nature, from the great body of thought surrounding us, unseen, but all powerful. This power is one of the strongest forces in nature, and if properly used will attract assistance from the most unexpected quarters. "Thoughts are Things," and possess a wonderful power of attracting to themselves other thought waves of the same vibratory pitch and quality.

4. By the power of thought in shaping your character and temperament to meet the requirements of your organization. You lack certain qualities needful for your success. You know it as well, if not better, than anyone else, but you have been deluded by a belief that these shortcomings were a part of you and that "the leopard cannot change his spots." To you the study of the Law of Mental Control comes as a might ally, for you can overcome these deficiencies, and can acquire new characteristics and qualities, as well as learning how to strengthen those which

you have already. I will endeavor to start you on the right road, by this series of lessons. I will print out the way for you, but you must do the work yourself. Every man must work out his own salvation in this study, as in every other branch of human endeavor.

Chapter 4

DIRECT PSYCHIC INFLUENCE

*Influence in a personal interview—The three great methods—Direct suggestion—
Thought waves—The adductive quality of thought—What is suggestion?—The Dual
Mind—Hypnotic Suggestion—The Active and Passive functions—The qualities of the
two functions—Human sheep—The two brother partners—The passive brother—The
active brother—Their respective traits—The "dead-easy" man—The "hard-as-nails
man—How to elude the vigilant partner—Never take No! for an answer, in business or
in love—Fortune is feminine—Love laughs at locksmiths—Confidence will win the day.*

In this and the next lesson I will endeavor to make plain to you the
process whereby an individual exerts an influence over his fellow men, in
a personal interview, and interests them in his schemes and plans; enlists
their aid and support; secures their patronage; and influences them generally. We all know men who are able to accomplish these results, and
yet we content ourselves with wondering about their strange power,
without endeavoring to acquire it.

The art of influencing men or women whilst we are in their presence,
of necessity includes the other several methods of mental influence mentioned in the preceding lessons, and partakes of the nature of each. It is
difficult to speak intelligently of this phase of mental influences, without
covering the entire grounds that will be explained in subsequent lessons.
I must content myself with a general reference to these several different
branches of the subject; as you will meet them later on, at which time I
will take them up at greater length. I would suggest that after complet-
ing this series of lessons you take up this particular lesson again, and go
over it carefully a second time. You will have a much clearer idea of this

subject, and many things which now seem more or less vague and unsatisfactory, will appear clear and easily understood.

In influencing men who we meet face to face, we affect them in a number of ways, which may be roughly summed up in three forms, viz.:

1. By direct suggestion through the voice, manner, appearance and eye. This includes not only voluntary suggestions on our part, but also the suggestions made involuntarily by every earnest man.

2. By thought waves directed to the other person by a voluntary effort of our mind.

3. By the adductive quality of thought, resulting from the process of controlled thought, of which I spoke in the preceding lesson. This force, once generated, operates involuntarily and constitutes the most striking phase of what we call Personal Magnetism.

In this lesson I shall confine myself to the first mentioned form of personal influence, and will take up the succeeding forms in subsequent lessons.

It is a most difficult task to give an intelligent comprehensive idea of the subject of Suggestion, in the limited space at my disposal. If the student has acquainted himself with the principles underlying Hypnotism or Hypnotic Suggestion, he will readily understand just what I mean when I say "Suggestion." To those who have not had this advantage, I will say that a suggestion is "an impression, consciously or unconsciously received through any of our senses." We are constantly accepting or rejecting suggestions, the acceptance or rejection depending upon the degree of suggestibility in ourselves, the degree being caused by the development or cultivation of the non-receptive qualities of the mind. We cannot attempt to go deeply into the subject of what is known as the Dual Mind in man, which has been variously designated as the Objective and Subjective minds; the Voluntary and involuntary minds; the Conscious and Subconscious minds, etc. If the student is desirous of acquainting himself fully with this subject, I would suggest that he take up some good work on Hypnotism or Hypnotic Suggestion. There are several good books on this subject, but I would suggest the occult books published by The Library Shelf (known as Series A, B, C, and D), which are courses of instruction in the basic principles of personal magnetism, hypnotism, suggestion and kindred branches of psychic research.

In order that the student may grasp the idea that I wish to convey regarding the use of suggestion as a means of exerting personal influence, I would have him understand that the mind has two general functions, which (following the terms used by me in my other writings) are known as the Active Function and the Passive Function, respectively. The Active function does the voluntary, volitional thinking, and also manifests what we call "will power." It is the function used frequently by the active, energetic, vigorous, wide-awake man, in his busy moments. The Passive function does the instinctive, automatic, and involuntary thinking, exhibiting no "will power" and manifesting on entirely contrary lines from the Active function. The Passive function is a most valuable servant on man, and really performs the greater part of his mental work, doing all the drudgery and fulfilling its allotted task without receiving praise or thanks. It works uncomplainingly, and apparently without any effort, and never seems to tire. The Active function, on the other hand, works only at the promptings of the will, and uses up a greater amount of nervous force than its Passive brother. It does the energetic active work of the mind, and tires after a great deal of effort and cries out for rest. You are conscious of, more or less, the effort when you employ the Active function, but not so when you use the easy going, faithful, good natured Passive function. I think that you will understand the distinctive features of these two functions, from this brief explanation.

Some persons do nearly all their thinking along Passive lines. Such persons find it too much of a task to do their own thinking, and prefer the "ready-made" thought of others, to that of their own production. They are practically human sheep. They are very credulous and will accept almost any statement made to them in an earnest, positive manner. These people are very suggestible and are practically at the mercy of those of a more active mind. They find it hard to say "No," and are inclined to say, "Yes," if it is easier and requires less thinking. Others are not quite so suggestible, and some are scarcely suggestible at all, at times. But the latter, when they relax and give their Active functions a rest, are much more suggestible than at other times.

To enable you to form a mental picture of the two functions, for the purpose of carrying out the instructions given in this course, I will ask you to imagine a pair of twins who are associated as partners in a business enterprise. They look exactly alike, but have very different qualities, and each one is well fitted for the performance of the special duties, which he has undertaken. They share equally in the profits and losses of the business. The Passive brother attends to receiving goods; filling orders; packing goods; keeping the stick in order, etc., while the Active brother financiering; pushing things along, and, in short, is the executive of the concern and its active spirit. When it comes to the buying of goods, however, both brothers take a hand.

The Passive brother is a good-natured, easygoing, "dead-easy" sort of fellow; a plodding, automatic, mechanical sort of man. He is somewhat "set" in his notions, rather superstitious and bigoted, but very credulous and apt to believe almost anything one may tell him, providing the new statement does not directly conflict with some of his preconceived notions. To get a radically new idea into his head it is necessary to "insinuate" it into him, by degrees. He is in the habit of deferring to the opinions of his brother, when the latter is around, and, in his brother's absence, to the opinions of other people. He will be apt to grant you any favor, to give you almost anything you ask, providing you make the request in a firm, confident manner. He is afraid of hurting your feelings by a refusal, and will promise you anything to get rid of you, and to avoid giving you a positive refusal. You can sell him almost anything if his brother is not watching him, if you go about it right. All you have to do is to put on a bold, confident front, and take things for granted. You know the type.

The Active brother, however, is a very different sort of a fellow. He is a suspicious, watchful, wide-awake, "hard as nails" sort of individual. There is no nonsense about him. He finds it necessary to keep a close watch on his Passive brother in order that the interests of the firm do not suffer. The Passive brother is always getting "stuck" by somebody, or on something, and really needs some sort of a guardian, and if the Active fellow happens to take a nap or be too busy with his work to keep an eye on the Passive brother, something is sure to happen to the latter. The Active partner, accordingly, is not inclined to allow you to meet the Passive brother, until he knows you pretty well, or thinks that you have no designs on the easy fellow. He watches you carefully and inquires into your business, and tries to find what you are up to, before he will allow you to see the other partner. If he thinks that you have designs on the easy fellow, he will tell you that his easy brother is out, etc. Even if he allows you to see his brother, he will watch every motion and listen to every word, and in the case he thinks that you are trying to play some sort of a game on the easy man, he will put his foot down on the scheme and call the deal off. He considers every proposition, and accepts it, if reasonable, or rejects it if not. He grows less suspicious when he becomes accustomed to your presence, and may even grow to have considerable confidence in you. He also may be entertained and amused, at which times he relaxes his vigilance and grows less suspicious. If his suspicions are once allayed, you may be able to get in a word with the other brother, in which case you have made a great advance, for the easy brothers, once acquainted with you, will himself contrive to make the next meeting easier. He feels lonesome and chafes under the restraint imposed upon him by his brother, and when he once makes your acquaintance he will be on the lookout for another chance to have a chat with you. The first step is the hardest.

Please remember that the mind of every man or woman is a partnership, composed of functions represented by the two characters with which I have just endeavored to acquaint you. There is a difference however in firms. The Passive partner is pretty much the same in all cases, although in some he manages to have his own way more, and in others he is kept still further in the background, the difference being caused by the degree of positive-ness in the Active partner. There is a great difference in these Active partners. Some of them are splendid examples of prudence, watchfulness and sagacity, whilst others possess these qualities in a lesser degree, and some are nearly as "easy" as their Passive brothers. Some of them can be "bulldozed," others coaxed, others flattered; and others tired out into relaxing their vigilance. Some of them get so interested in something that they do not notice that the visitor is getting well acquainted with the Passive brother, and may even allow him to give an order for goods. Each one has his own peculiarities, his weaknesses. As a man is no stronger that his weakest point, to obvious rule is to find that weakest point and direct the attack right there. You will readily see that the main thing to be accomplished is to elude the vigilance of the Active partner. There are many ways of doing this—the thing to do is to find out the best way. If one way does not work, try another. If you keep at it you will win eventually. "Faint heart never won fair lady." It can be done if it is gone about properly. It is done every day. It is easy with some, and hard with others, but it can be done with all of these watchful partners if you will only keep pecking away at it.

Never take "No" for an answer. Pursue the same plan in business that you would if you were courting the girl you loved. In the latter case, a "No" or two, or a dozen for that matter, would not count. Pursue the same tactics in your business, and you will win the day. Fortune is feminine, you know, and possesses all of the characteristics of the sex.

Suggestions gain force by repletion. A man may reject a proposition when first made, but upon hearing the same thing over and over again, he will come to believe it. No wonder, you believe it yourself from the mere repletion of it, and why shouldn't he. Moreover, a suggestion may produce no apparent effect at the time it is given, but may be like the seed planted in fertile soil, which will have sprouted by the time you come again. By talking properly to the Active partner and getting him interested you have enabled the passive brother, actuated by curiosity (of which he has a full share) to draw near and overhear your conversation. He will often think over the overheard words after you have gone, and the next time you come he will manage to get an interview with you, in spite of his stern brother. "Love laughs at locksmiths," and so does the Passive fellow at his brother—sometimes. You should carry the above mental picture of the two functions of the mind—the Active partner and his Passive brother. With this picture in your mind, you will be able to direct your suggestions to the best advantage, and also to guard yourself against the suggestions of others.

In influencing a man with whom you come in personal contact, you will not have to depend entirely upon the power of suggestion in overcoming the watchfulness of the Active partner of his mind. You will be aided by two powerful allies, i.e., direct thought waves consciously projected by your mind, and by the involuntary addictive qualities of thought. These powers can be highly developed by the exercises, which will be given you during this course of lessons. You will also learn how to acquire characteristics calculated to aid you in making a good impression upon the Active brother, who is apt to be impressed by external appearances.

There is one thing, which you must learn, however, and that is Confidence and a belief in your ability to master this subject. It is like a boy learning to swim. The swimming power is inherent in every boy, but he doesn't believe it. As soon as he believes that he can swim—he swims; but so long as he believes that he "can't"—he cannot. He may improve in the art of swimming by practice, but he had the swimming power in him from the beginning, and all he needed was belief. You can do it, and have but to strike out. You can begin on easy exercises at first, but you must have Confidences from the start. Some men discover this by accident, and do not know the reason for their success. You know the reason, now, and can do as well and better than the man who has stumbled upon the truth.

Chapter 5

A LITTLE WORLDLY WISDOM

How to influence the Active partner—Conversation—The art of listening—Carlyle and his visitor—A delightful conversation—Keep yourself positive—Appearance—Apparel— Clean linen—Perfumes—Cleanliness—Manner—Reserve—Temper—Fearlessness— Self-Respect—Consideration for others—Frankness—Earnestness—Firm handshake— The eye—Tone of voice—A useful rule—How to remedy deficiencies in manner.

In the preceding lesson I compared the two functions of the mind of each individual, to the two brothers—partners in a business enterprise. For the convenience of explanation, I will continue this illustration, which is quite applicable to the real state of affairs.

This Active partner is a "particular" old fellow, and needs considerable humoring, and careful handling. He is influenced, to some extent, by the conversation, appearance, manner, voice, eye, etc., and each Active partner has his own tastes and peculiarities, although there are some things, which they all have in common. As to conversation, we should if possible ascertain what interests, but do not make the mistake of talking too much. "Give the old man a chance." You should talk until you get him well started on a favorite topic, and then you keep quiet. You should cultivate the art of listening, for it is one of the most valuable accomplishments in the world. Many a man (or woman) has risen to a high position simply by being a good listener. You may remember the old tale told of Thomas Carlyle. A visitor once called on him, and being a good listener and a student of human nature as well, managed to get him started talking on a favorite subject. Carlyle talked for over three hours without giving the visitor "a chance to get a word in edgewise." When the caller at last rose to depart, Carlyle accompanied him to the door, in a surprisingly good humor, and bade him good-bye saying, "Come again, Mon., we've had a most delightful conversation." Do you see the point? Listen attentively to the old Active partner, and act as if each of his words was a bright golden dollar, fresh from the mint—but do not fall under the influence of his spell. Pay earnest attention to what he says, but do not let his thoughts produce any real impression upon you, or else he will be selling goods to you, Passive partner. Keep yourself positive, not negative, for you will have a word to say to the easy brother after the old fellow becomes "intoxicated with the exuberance of his own verbosity," and relaxes his vigilance. By all means cultivate the art of intelligent listening.

As to appearance, I would advise you to avoid the two extremes of flashiness and dowdiness, respectively. Keep in the middle of the road. You should particularly avoid clothing calculated to attract special attention, either by its extreme style or the reverse. The apparel should be simple, neat and clean. Do not wear a shabby hat or muddy, shabby shoes. To this effect, even a fine suit of clothes is lost. Always wear clean linen. These things count. Eschew the use of strong perfumes. To most men, strong perfumes are an abomination. It is scarcely necessary to add that personal cleanliness is an important prerequisite for obtaining a favorable hearing with the majority of Active partners, even though they may not be too particular themselves. Your manner should be pleasant and cheerful, yet not frivolous. A certain degree of reserve is desirable. Your temper, of course, should be well under control. Anger is a sign of weakness—not strength, and the angry man is always placed at a disadvantage. You should be absolutely fearless, both physically and morally, the latter being the rarer quality. If you are quick tempered, or apt to give way to fear of misfortune, or worry, etc., you should pay particular attention to the lesson on Character Building, and correct these defects.

Your manner should convey the idea of self-respect, but should likewise show a delicate consideration for the likes and dislikes of others. If you lack the latter quality, you should cultivate it by all means, as it is of paramount importance in creating friends and in gaining the favor of Active partners, the latter being only human in spite of their rough exteriors. If you will carry in your mind this thought: "I act toward you as I would like you to act toward me," and make the thought take form in action, you will acquire this valuable quality.

Cultivate a frank, open manner. Most people like it. Be earnest when you talk. It not only holds the attention of the people to whom you are talking, but is a valuable aid to you in having your suggestions accepted, and, besides, is an important factor in imparting force to your thought vibrations. Cultivate a firm, honest, manly handshake. Nobody likes to have thrust upon him a flabby limp hand. You don't yourself. Do not forget this. If you have not the proper handshake, start to work and get it at once. Shake hands with everyone as if he were your best girl's millionaire father. And then look people square in the eye. I will have more to say about the power of the eye, in the next lesson, but I wish to call your attention to it in connection with the hearty handshake. The two go together.

Cultivate an agreeable tone of voice, avoiding a mumbling utterance on the one hand, and a loud boisterous tone on the other. An excellent rule is to pitch the voice to the tone of the party with whom you are conversing, providing always that you do not shout in order to keep pace with the other person. If the other man shouts, keep you own voice even and subdued, and he will soon drop to your pitch. This, by the way, is a good plan to adopt with a person who is excited and is attempting to give you a good "tongue lashing." In such a case keep your temper and see that your voice is subdued and steady, and you will find the voice of the other man (or woman) gradually dropping down to your pitch. As he lowers his voice his temper subsides, and he feels ashamed, and you have won the day. Try it. There is much in the voice. A flexible, well-modulated voice is most pleasing, and wins many victories for its fortunate possessor. Let your voice express the shade of feeling, which you wish to convey. This is one of the most potent forms of suggestion. An expressive voice is one of the principal tools of the successful suggestionist.

The student must not despair if he lacks some of the important requisites to success above mentioned. He should know that every one of these gifts is within his reach, if he will but take the trouble to acquire it. I explain this point fully in Character Building.

Another very important medium of influencing others, including our old Active partner, is the Eye. The Human Eye! Who does not know its power, and yet how few know how to acquire the secret offense and defense, and its aid in influencing man and the lower animals, and yet not begin to exhaust the subject. I will devote our next lesson to an explanation of the use of the eye as an influencing medium; how to acquire the "magnetic gaze"; and how to avoid the influence of the eyes of others.

Chapter 6

THE POWER OF THE EYE

The most potent means of influencing others—The reasons—The trained eye, a powerful weapon—Mental vibrations conveyed by the eye—Its power over wild beast and savages—Steady gaze almost unbearable—Proper use of the eye—Fascination and hypnotic attraction—The magnetic gaze—The beginning of the interview—How to use the eye to command attention—How to hold attention—How to regain attention—Get what you want before you leave—Self-protection—How to prevent others from influencing you—How to say "No!"—How to give suggestions.

The eye is one of the most potent means of influencing others. It not only serves to hold the attention of the person to whom you are talking, thereby rendering it easier to impress your suggestions upon him; but it is also a power in itself, which when properly used is the means of impressing your will upon another. It attracts, fascinates, and holds spellbound the Active partner, and gives you a chance to talk with the easygoing brother. The eye of the man, who has mastered the law of mental control, is a powerful weapon. It conveys the strong mental vibrations direct to the mind of the other party, at short range. You have heard of the power of the human eye over wild beast and savages, and many of you have met with men who seemed to look clear through you and whose steady gaze was almost unbearable. I will give you a few exercises, in our next lesson, which will aid you in acquiring what is known as the "magnetic gaze," a most important acquisition for the student of personal influence. In this lesson, I will assume that you have already acquired the "magnetic gaze." The proper use of the eye, in interviews with other persons, will enable you to exert an influence over them something akin to fascination or hypnotic attraction. This is the result of strong mental vibrations conveyed at short range by means of the magnetic gaze of the trained eye.

You, of course will be governed by the circumstances of each particular case, and it is difficult to give you general directions applicable to all cases. You must adapt these general instructions to suit the emergence of each particular case as it arises.

One of the most important things about the beginning of an interview is that you should look the other person squarely in the eye, with a firm, steady "magnetic gaze." You need not stare at him, but your gaze must be steady and firm, and indicative of strong will power and concentration. During the conversations you may change the direction of your gaze, but whenever you make a proposition, statement or request, or whatever you wish to impress him strongly, you must direct a firm, steady magnetic gaze towards him, looking him straight in the eye. This is highly important and must not be neglected. When you are talking business, have an earnest, determined look or manner and hold the other man's attention. If you have a request to make, make it in a clear, dignified, earnest manner, keeping your eyes fixed upon his, and willing at the same time that he will do as you say. By all means prevent him from looking away from you at this point. You must hold his attention at all hazards. If you have his whole attention, the Active brother, will be too engrossed to bother about his easy brother, and the latter will draw near and hear what you are saying. If the other party avoids your gaze, you can sometimes regain his attention by looking away yourself (watching him all the time out of the corner of your eye) and as soon as he finds that you are looking the other way he will be opt to steal a glance at you. You must watch for this stolen glance, and the moment you find his eye turned towards your face you must quickly turn you eye and give a quick, sharp determined look, keeping your eyes fastened upon his, and holding his look by an effort of the will. Right there is a good point for you to drive in your little nail. You have him at a disadvantage, and the psychological moment has arrived for driving in a strong suggestion.

If you cannot get him to look at you in the way above mentioned, it is a very good plan to have something to show him; a sample, picture, or some other object ascertaining to your business. You will find that after he looks at the object shown him, he will raise his eyes to yours. He will do this every time, and you must be ready for him with a firm, magnetic gaze and a strong suggestion. If you can keep a mans attention, and can manage to look squarely at him during the interview, you will surely influence him to a greater or lesser extent; unless he is well posted on this subject in which case it will be very difficult to influence him by direct means. Very few people, however, possess this knowledge and you need not figure that element into the ordinary calculation. You may find that the other man will begin to feel that you are gaining some sort of influence over him, and he may in self-defense endeavor to terminate the interview. This you must not permit, for you have gained an influence and you must follow it up. Do not leave him until you get what you came for.

In this connection it may be well to suggest to you that, inasmuch as it is difficult for anyone to reason or deliberate clearly whilst they are under the influence of the magnetic gaze of another, it will be well for you to guard yourself against the use of this power at the hands of anyone else possessing the secret. You must preserve a positive mental attitude when you find that someone is trying to influence you, and hold the thought, firmly, that you are strong and beyond such influence. This mental attitude will protect you and you must, of course, reverse the instructions given you for influencing others. If a man is endeavoring to interest you in a proposition, do not allow him to hold your gaze uninterruptedly during the conversation. You may without seeming to avoid his gaze, look away reflectively at intervals, in an easy way. This will give you time to reflect a little, and maintain your balance. When he makes you a proposition, look away from him in a deliberative manner as if you are carefully considering every word that he is saying. If he manages to drive in a sudden suggestion, or proposition, when he holds your eye, do not answer him until you have taken your eyes away for a minute and regained your positive balance. Then, if your answer is "No," look him square in the eye with a positive glance and say your "No," firmly and deliberately, but of course politely. When in doubt, say "No." Keep a sharp lookout for insidious suggestion given at a psychological moment, for this is where much of the danger lies. Let your own "Active partner" be alive to his duties and do not let the other fellow get in a word with your Passive partner. They will want to get a word with each other, but you must put down your Active foot on it. The man, who is doing the talking, if he understands his business, always is the positive factor in a conversation, whilst the listener is more or less passive. The more intently and earnestly he listens, the more passive he is. The positive is stronger than the negative, and people should always be on their guard to avoid having positives suggestions forced upon them when they are in a negative condition.

You should learn to give suggestions in an earnest, firm; positive manner, your voice showing that you expect them to be acted upon, and your mind assuming the belief that such will be the case. If you have not this desirable quality you should take a few lessons from some good suggestors, and practice on his subjects. The experience thus gained will be most useful. It is almost impossible to convey in a written lesson the manner and tone of voice best adapted for this purpose, which information I always impart to my personal classes by means of actual experiments, under my supervision. If you will form a mental picture of what is implied by the two words Confident Earnestness, you will be able to grasp the idea I intend to convey when I tell you to make your suggestions "in the proper manner." The lesson on Concentration will also aid you in the respect Our next lesson will be devoted to the "Magnetic Gaze."

Chapter 7

The Magnetic Gaze

What is the magnetic gaze—Full explanation of exercises—How to acquire the magnetic gaze—An interesting study—People will manifest fear—Experiment on "live subjects"—Exercise 1: Full directions for acquiring the firm, steady gaze—Remarkable achievements—A masterful expression—Effects on men and animal—Exercise 2: Mirror exercises for developing the gaze—How to withstand the gaze of others—Exercise 3: Rolling gaze—Exercise 4: Strengthening the nerves and muscles of the eye—Exercise 5: Experiments on others—Trial on animals—Animals will move away—Men unpleasantly affected—Proper use of the power—Keep your own secrets.

What is known as the Magnetic Gaze is the expression of a strong mental demand, by means of the eye whose nerves and muscles have been trained for the work, and which is thereby enabled to maintain a firm, steady, positive gaze. The production of the mental effort will be explained in a subsequent lesson, and we will now speak only of the eye itself. The following exercises are very important, and I trust that the student will closely follow the same. By the practice you will so develop this faculty that few will be able to withstand your gaze. This is a most interesting study, and you will have the pleasure of seeing the increase of the power of your eye manifested by the people with whom you come in contact. You will soon find that people will become restless and uneasy beneath your gaze, and some will manifest indications of something akin to fear, if you concentrate your gaze upon them for a few seconds. When once you have mastered this accomplishment and have acquired the strong magnetic gaze, you would not part with your gift for a large sum of money. You should not content yourself with merely performing the exercises given below, but should experiment on persons with whom you come in contact, and note the results. You can acquire a perfect working knowledge of the power of the eye, only by experiment upon "live subjects."

Exercises

Exercise 1. Take a piece of white writing paper about six inches square, upon which you have drawn a circle about the size of a silver quarter-dollar, the circle then being filled in with black ink so that the spot will stand out black and distinct upon the white background. Pin the paper upon the wall at about the height of your eyes when are seated. Place you chair in the middle of the room and seat yourself directly facing the paper. Fix your eyes steadily upon the black spot, and gaze at it firmly, without winking, for one minute. After resting the eyes, practice the exercise again. After resting the eyes, practice the exercise again. Repeat five times. With the chair in its original place, move your paper three feet to the right of its original position. Seat yourself and fix your gaze on the wall directly in front of you, then, without moving the head, cast the eyes to the right and gaze steadily at the spot for one minute. Repeat four times.

Then, placing the paper on the wall three feet to the left of its original position, gaze steadily at the spot for one minute. Repeat five times. Continue this exercise for three days, and then increase the time of the gaze to two minutes. At the end of three more days, increase the time to three minutes; and so on, increasing the time in one-minute increments every three days. Some persons have acquired the power of gazing steadily for twenty to thirty minutes, without winking or having their eyes fill with water, but I do not advise extending the limit beyond fifteen minutes. The man, who can maintain the gaze for fifteen minutes, can direct as powerful a gaze as he who has attained the thirty-minute record.

This exercise is the most important one, and, if faithfully followed up, will enable you to gaze steadily and earnestly at anyone with whom you are talking. It will impart a strong, masterful expression to the eye, and enable you to maintain a steady gaze, which few will be able to withstand. Dogs and other animals will quail before your gaze, and its effect will manifest itself also in numerous other ways. The practice of the exercises is somewhat tedious, but anyone will be amply repaid for the time and trouble bestowed upon it. If you are practicing hypnotism, you will find this gaze most helpful to you. It will have the further effect of causing the eye to appear fuller, by increasing the space between the eyelids.

Exercise 2. You may supplement the first exercise with the following, which will add variety, relieve the monotony, and accustom you to gaze into the eyes of others without embarrassment. Stand in front of your mirror and gaze into the reflection of your own eyes, in the manner mentioned in Exercise No. 1. Increase the time as in the previous exercise. This exercise will accustom you to bear the gaze of others, and also will enable you to obtain the best expression of the eye, and in other ways will be useful to you. It will enable you to see the growth and development of the characteristic expression of your eye when it is acquiring the magnetic gaze. By all means practice this exercise, systematically. Some authorities prefer this exercise to the preceding one, but, in my opinion, the best results are obtained by a combination of the two.

Exercise 3. Stand erect, facing the wall at a distance of three feet. Place your sheet of paper in front of you, with the spot directly in front of the eyes. Fix your gaze upon the spot, and then move your head around in a circle, keeping your gaze fixed upon the spot. As this exercise causes the eyes to roll around and keeping the gaze steady, the nerves and muscles receive considerable exercise. Vary the exercise by circling the head in different directions. Use the exercise mildly at first, and avoid tiring the eyes.

Exercise 4. Stand with you back against the wall, and, facing toward the opposite wall, shift your gaze rapidly from one point of the wall to another—right, left, up, down, zigzag, circle, etc. This exercise should be discontinued when the eyes begin to feel tired, the best plan for concluding the exercise being to gaze intently at one point, which will rest the eyes after the previous motion. This exercise is calculated to strengthen the muscles and nerves of the eye.

Exercise 5. After having acquired a firm gaze, you will gain confidence by persuading a friend to allow you to practice your gaze upon him. Place your friend in a chair opposite your own; sit down and gaze calmly, steadily and firmly into his eyes, instructing him to look at you as long as he can. You will find that you will easily tire him out, and that by the time he cries "enough" he will be in an almost hypnotic condition. If you have a hypnotic subject, he (or she) will answer still better. You also may try the strength of your gaze on a dog, cat or other animal, provided that you are able to induce it to stand still or lie still. You will find, however, that most animals will move away, or turn the head, in order to avoid you steady gaze.

You of course will distinguish between a steady, calm gaze, and an impudent stare. The first is indicative of the man of strong psychical power whilst the latter denotes the cad.

You will find, at first, that your strong, steady gaze may somewhat disconcert those with whom you come in contact, and may embarrass those at whom you are directing your gaze, causing them to become uneasy and "rattled" You will soon accustom yourself to your new power, and will use it discreetly, so as to avoid embarrassment to others whilst producing an effect on them.

I would caution you against discussing or speaking of your eye exercises, or practice of Personal Magnetism, to others, as that course would result only in making people suspicious of you, and in other ways proving a serious detriment to the proper use of your powers of influencing people. Keep your own secrets, and let your force manifest itself by results, not by boasting. In addition to these reasons, there are good occult reasons why you should keep your own council about your new accomplishments. A neglect to observe this advice will be a source of regret to you. Take your time in practicing these exercises, and do not rush things unduly. Follow Nature's rule and develop your power gradually but surely.

Chapter 8

THE VOLIC FORCE

Distinction between the adductive Quality of Thought and the Volic Force—Varying manifestations of thought vibrations—Definition of Volation and Volic Force—A most potent force—The real man—The "I Am"—Its recognition—Its importance—Man attains hitherto unknown powers—The Soul of Man—The will—The secret of the development of the will—Active and Passive mentation—The projection of thought waves.

In the preceding lessons, I have given you an explanation of the manner whereby one person may attract another, in a personal interview, by means of the power of suggestion, etc. The person thus making the impression upon another is aided in his work by two other forces. The first of these assisting forces is what is known as the Adductive Quality of Thought, of which I will speak in subsequent lessons; the second is the Volative influence of the mind of one person over the mind of another. There is a marked difference in these two manifestations of the power of the mind. In the first instances, the Adductive Quality of Thought, once being set in motion, affects others without a conscious effort of your mind; your mere thinking strongly of certain things, setting a mighty force in motion which influences others. In the case of Volation, the mental vibrations are sent out and impelled by the conscious exercise of the will power of the sender, and are directed toward some special object; when the impelling power is withdrawn, the vibrations cease.

I find no term in general use, which is especially applicable to this form of thought force, and I do not desire to continue to speak of it as "the conscious effort of the will, producing thought-vibrations, and impelling the same toward a given object." I am driven, by necessity, to the coining of a name to express this idea. I shall, accordingly, hereafter use the term Volation, to indicate the idea above defined, the said word being derived from the Latin word *Volos*, the will. This word must not be confounded with Volition, meaning the free exercise of the will in making a choice. I shall also use the term *volic* (from the same source), meaning "of the will." The Volic power is one of nature's most potent forces, and at the same time is the least understood. It is exerted, more or less, unconsciously by all men. Some are aware of its effects without understanding the laws of its production and development. It may be greatly increased by intelligent practice and training, if one will devote to the task the necessary time and effort. I will give you exercises for the proper development of this power, in the lesson on Concentration.

To be able to make intelligent use of the Volic Force, it is necessary to understand the real nature of the will; and to understand the real nature of the will; you must realize what is the real *man*.

Many of us have been in the habit of thinking of the Ego—the "I" of ourselves—as merely the physical body. This is the materialistic point of view. Others think of their "I" as a mental creature having control of the body, and having his abode in the brain. This is partially correct, but is only half the truth. Others realize that there is a "higher self" in the man, and a few have recognized that "higher self," and live in accord with its dictates. The real Ego, or "I," is as much higher than Mind, as Mind is higher than the body; and both body and mind are subordinate to it. Both are its tools and are used for its work, when it sees fit to use them. The real self is that which we feel when in times of reverie and introspection, we think or say, "I AM." All of us have felt this consciousness of the real self, at certain times in our lives, but have failed to realize its full importance. Lay down this book for a few moments, and, relaxing the muscles of your body and assuming a passive state of mind, think quietly and calmly on the words "I AM," and endeavor to picture your real self, superior to both mind and body. If you have secured the proper state of mind and body, you will perceive a glimmer of the presence of the real self within you. Continue the practice. It will awaken in your mind a perception of the truth. Nothing can injure or destroy the real self. The body and mind may pass away, but the "I AM" is eternal, and impregnable to harm. It is powerful, and, when the mind has learned to adapt itself to its influence, man becomes like another being, and acquire hither to unknown powers.

The purpose of this series of lessons does not permit me to dwell at length upon this subject. Its importance demands a work of many volumes to do it even faint justice, but I wish, at this point, to direct the attention of the student to this vital truth, with all the earnestness of which I am capable. Take whatever view you wish regarding the instructions given you in this course, accept its teachings or reject them, as you see fit, but let this one thought sink deeply into your mind: *The I am is your real self.* When your mind recognizes its master, you will have learned the secret of Life. I have planted this thought seed in you mind, and it will grow and evolve into a beautiful plant bearing a flower whose fragrance will surpass that of earth's fairest blossoms. When its leaves unfold and show the flower in all its beauty, then will you know that you have found yourself.

Lord of a thousand worlds am I,
And I reign since time began;
And night and day, in cyclic sway,
Shall pass while their deeds I scan.
Yet time shall cease ere I find release,
For I am the soul of man.

(Charles H. Orr)

That which we mean when we say "the will" is a manifestation of; the I AM of the individual, bearing nearly the same relation to it that thought it does to the mind. When we speak of "developing the will," we really mean the developing of the mind to recognize and be controlled by the will. The will is strong enough; it does not need "developing." This is contrary to the generally accepted doctrine, but is it correct, nevertheless. A strong will current is flowing over the psychic wires, but you must learn to raise the trolley pole to the wire, before you are able to move the mental car.

Man thinks along different lines. One class of thinking which we have called Passive Mentation is little more than instinctive effort—it sort of "thinks itself," and requires little or no Volic Force for its production. Another class of mental effort, which we will call Active Mentation, is produced by a greater or lesser demand of the mind upon the power of the will. I can merely call your attention to this fact, as a detailed treatment of the matter is without the scope of this work. I have gone deeper into you. In this work I am called upon to teach "How" and not "Why," and, therefore, I do not care to take you beyond the border of the realm of theory. The more man thinks along the lines of Active Mentation, the stronger and more forceful are his thoughts. The reverse is, of course, likewise true. The man who understands the law of Mental Control is placed at the immense advantage over his brother, who follows the "calf path" of Passive mental effort.

Thoughts of all kinds are projected by the mind, and their vibrations go out from the individual, influencing others to a greater or lesser degree, according to the force of the impelling effort. Passive thoughts are less powerful than active thoughts, but the former, if constantly repeated, have much force. It will be seen, readily, that in order to produce a direct effect upon the mind of another by thought vibrations, an effort of Volation is required; the stronger the effort, the stronger the effect.

The next lesson will be devoted to the subject of the exercise of the power of Volation.

Chapter 9

DIRECT VOLATION

Volation, the measure of success—Leaders of men possess it—Unconscious acquirement—Napoleon Bonaparte aware of the truth—Strong men feel the "I"—Desire—Some not willing to "pay the price" of success—Men who have mastered occult power—The vibratory force—Telepathy, thought transference and mind reading—Masters of the art guard their secrets—The prime requisite for acquirement—Exercise of volation in personal interview—Expectation—Some men but puppets—General instructions—Power must not be used to harm others—A warning—Satan's terrible example—How to "will" a thing—Exercise 1: Making a person turn around—Exercise 2: Influencing a person in a public place—Exercise 3: Influencing a person without looking directly at him—Comical results—Exercise 4: Suggesting a forgotten word—Remarkable results obtained by a German student—Exercise 5: Directing the motions of another person—Exercise 6: Window exercises—Influencing passers-by—Fascinating experiments—To be used for your own development, not for amusement or to satisfy vulgar curiosity.

The exercise of Volation differs very materially, in degree, among different men. It maybe states, broadly, that a man exerts an influence over other men in an exact ratio to his measure of Volation. The ledger of men has developed this power to a comparatively high degree, although perhaps unconsciously and without any knowledge of the workings of the mighty force which is operating in his behalf. Many such men frankly admit that they are unable to explain or account for their power over men. They know that they have some sort of power, but are ignorant of its nature or laws. Napoleon is a striking example of a man of highly developed Volation. His will was imposed upon millions of men who obeyed his commands, and he accomplished results little short of miraculous. From remarks dropped by him, it seems probable that he had, at least, a faint idea of the force at his command, and he acted in accordance therewith, for a while. He afterwards attempted to misuse his power; lost sight of the source of his strength; neglected its laws, and fell. You will notice that all successful men instinctively feel the "I" strongly. They have faith in themselves, and frequently feel that they have a special Providence overlooking their affairs. They, like Napoleon, feel that they have a "star of destiny." This is an instinctive recognition of the I AM. They have but a glimpse of the truth, and have made the most of it, their strong desire for power, fame, or riches pushing them on, and causing them to instinctively avail themselves of the powerful aid of the Ego. There are many who recognize the power of the I AM, some of whom understand its laws, and yet these men do not assert themselves in the struggle for material reward. They have the power within them, but *desire* is not there. They are content with the lesser material rewards, and are not willing to "pay the price" of what is known as Success or the mastery of men. Many men who have mastered the occult power, scorn wealth, position and fame, and exert no desire for them, feeling that these things are unworthy of their power, and preferring to use the forces at their command for what they consider higher aims. They say with the prophet, "Vanity, vanity, all is vanity," and with Puck, "what fools these mortals be." The law of compensations seems to even all things, and wealth, power and position do not always bring happiness. The old sayings: "uneasy the head that wears the crown," and "There is no rose without its thorn," are literally true.

However, I do not propose preaching a sermon on Life, nor do I wish to point at moral. Every individual must choose for himself, and no man can decide for another. I say, however, that whatever you do, do it right. There is only one way to do things, and that is to do them. You must "put your hand to the plow, and look not backward." Select your goal and then move straight toward it, sweeping from your path all obstacles. To accomplish your aim, you must have Desire strongly present, and much recognize your real self, the I AM, in order to exert what is generally known as "will power," in the furtherance of your plans.

In the preceding lesson I have defined Volation as "the conscious effort of the will, producing thought vibrations and impelling them toward a given object." The vibratory force may be exerted in the ordinary way—at short range, upon the occasion of a personal interview; it may also be exerted in a much less understood way, by means of long-range vibrations (sometimes called telepathy). The first form is quite common, and we all have seen exhibitions of it; the second form is somewhat rare, and those who understand it best have but little to say about it. It is practiced quietly, however, by many more person than we usually dream of in that connection. We see mild examples of it in what is known as Telepathy or Thought Transference, mind Reading, etc., but those who understand the subject very imperfectly usually give these exhibitions. I know several persons who have developed this power to a wonderful degree, and in no case will they consent to an exhibition of their power to any but a few chosen friends, with whom they are in perfect sympathy and who happen to be likewise familiar with the subject. These people know the real nature of the power of which they are making use, and will not degrade it by making it the subject of an ordinary show. They are content with their knowledge and seek to convince no one else. The are not looking for converts, and, in fact, discourage any attempt to make public their occult knowledge believing that the time is not yet ripe for such publicity, and that its promulgation at this time would result in its misuse.

The prime requisite for the acquirement of the art of Volation is the recognition of the power of the real self—the I AM. The more complete the recognition, the greater the power. I cannot give you specific directions for acquiring this faculty of recognition. You must feel it rather that reason it out. You will not be in doubt as to whether you are on the right track—you will realize it at once. As near as I can express it to you, is to say that you will feel that your body is as a suit of clothes, which, whilst covering you temporarily, its not YOU; that you are separate and apart from your body and superior to it, although for the time being connected with it. You will realize that even your mind is not YOU, but that is merely the instrument through which YOU manifest yourself, and which being imperfect, prevents the complete expression of your real self. In short, when you say or think "I AM," you are conscious of the existence of your real self, and feel the growth of a new sense of power within you. This recognition of the self may be but faint; but encourage it and it will grow, and whilst growing will manifest itself to your mind by impressing upon the latter the knowledge of the proper plan for further development. It is an example of "to him who hath shall be given, and to him who hast not shall be taken away even that which he hath." Their mere calling of the attention to the act may awaken the recognition in some, whilst others will find it necessary to reflect upon the idea and awaken to recognition of the truth more slowly. Some will not feel the truth. To such I say: the time is not yet ripe for your recognition of this great truth, but the seed is planted and the plant will appear in time. This may seem like the veriest nonsense to you now but the time will come when you will admit its literal correctness. To those who feel the first indications of the awakening of the real self, I say: Carry the thought with you and it will unfold like the lotus, naturally and gradually; the truth once recognized cannot be lost, and there is no standing still in nature. To those who recognize the truth, I would like to say more, but this is not the place.

The practice of concentration, as explained in a subsequent lesson, will enable anyone to develop this idea of the real self. The thought, "I AM," held in the Silence, whilst you are concentrating, will grow stronger and stronger.

To exercise the power of Volation in influencing others, in a personal interview, you have merely to make a strong mental demand of the other person, accompanied with a consciousness of your right to do so, and the veil that your command will be obeyed. You must fully expect that your command will be obeyed. In all mental processes the earnest expectation is a prime factor in producing the effect. If you have only a faint, half-hearted expectation, you will have only halfway results. You will realize the reason for this after you have completed this course, the matter being explained in subsequent lessons.

Now, do not understand that you will be able to approach anyone, and by simply willing and expecting the results, make that person do just what you will. You could do all of this if the person had no power of mental resistance, no Volic Force of his own to counteract yours. Some persons, unfortunately for themselves, have but little Volic Forces, and are but puppets in the hands of those who know the secret of personal influence; others have a little more of the force, and so on, until the high stages are reached.

I do say, however, that you will obtain some degree of success from this plan from every person with whom you come in contact, the degree of success depending entirely upon the degree of Volic Force of the other person, as compared with you own. You will understand this well after a few trials. Do not hesitate in commencing to practice this form of mental influence at once. You will improve by practice, and will grasp the theory better from having put it into practice. Remember the boy not being able to swim until he believed he could, and tried. You should of course use Volation in connection with the power of suggestion as explained in preceding lessons. You will be able to concentrate your powers of command by observing the exercises given in the lesson on Concentration.

In other lessons, I will explain why these occult powers should not be used for any evil purposes or in working harm to anyone, but I think it well, at this point to caution students against any misuse of this power. Such practices, besides being wrong morally, will result to the disadvantage of the practitioner, and if persisted in, will wreck his prospects in the end. He may be successful temporarily but the result in the end will be disastrous. There are good occult reasons for this, and I hope that my warnings will be heeded by anyone reading this course. There is no harm in using this knowledge and information toward promoting your legitimate business interests and your welfare, providing always that no harm is inflicted on the person influenced. You may influence a man to deal with you, and if you treat him fairly, you are making no misuse of your powers. But, on the other hand, if you should influence a man for the purpose of swindling or cheating him or doing him other harm, you commit a great working for which you will some day suffer in proportion to the wrong perpetrated. I am not speaking of punishment in a future life, but right here in this world. "As ye sow so shall reap," holds well in this case. There is very little likelihood of your misusing your powers of Volation, for when you attain them fully; you will instinctively recoil from the idea of working evil by means of your newfound strength. There are, however, a few men in the world, who, like Satan, use their mighty power for evil, but, like Satan, these men are doomed to extreme misery and unhappiness. They are like fallen gods.

The best exercise for the development of Volation is of course Concentration, but it may be interesting to the student to be able to "try his hand" on a few simple tests so as to gain confidence in himself. I append a few exercises for this purpose. Many others will readily occur to the student. Try only easy tests at first, and then gradually work up to more difficult feats. Practice makes perfect.

Let me say here that when you "will" anything, do not get the notion that you must frown or clinch your fists or anything of that sort. The force is attained by a calm, undisturbed attitude, the "willing" being done in the form of a clam, earnest demand, and the thought that what you expect will occur. The earnest expectation is the secret. You will soon get the "knack" of it. Do not be discouraged, but keep at it until you get things working smoothly.

In our next lesson we will take up the subject of "long-range" Volation or, more properly, Telepathic Volation.

Exercise 1. Whilst walking down the street, fix your attention upon someone walking just ahead of you. A distance of at least six to ten feet should separate you, and a greater distance is no obstacle. Fasten a firm, steady, earnest gaze upon your subject, focusing the gaze upon the back of the neck, just at the base of the brain. Whilst gazing firmly at this point, will that the subject shall turn his head and look around in your direction. A little practice is required to perfect yourself in this exercise, but after you once acquire the "knack" of it, you will be surprised at the percentage of people whom you can affect in this way. Women seem to be more highly susceptible to this mental influence than are men.

Exercise 2. Fix your gaze upon some one sitting ahead of you in church, theater, concert, etc., focusing your gaze upon the same point as in the previous exercise, and will that the person shall look around. You will notice that the subject will fidget around in his seat, appear more or less uncomfortable, and finally half turn in his seat and direct a quick glance in your direction. This experiment will prove more successful with persons whom you know, than with strangers. The better you know the person, the quicker the influence will manifest itself. The two exercise just given can be indefinitely multiplied by the ingenuity of the student. The principle is the same in all cases, the concentrated gaze and strong, earnest, expectant willing or demanding the result, being the prime factors in producing the phenomenon. You, of course, realize that the concentrated will power can be developed by the practice of the exercises given in the lesson on Concentration. If you find difficulty in producing the above results, you will know that your powers of concentration are not sufficiently developed, and you will accordingly perfect yourself in this respect.

Exercise 3. Select some person who may be seated on the opposite side of a bus or train from you, but several seats to the right or left of the point directly opposite you. You may look straight ahead, so as to appear as if you were not looking at the other party, but you will be conscious of his presence, and will see him out of the corner of your eye. Direct a strong mental demand toward him, willing and expecting that he will look in your direction. If you manage it properly, you will find that in a few moments the party will suddenly glance in your direction. Sometimes the glance will be directed in a seemingly unconscious manner, just as if the party had merely felt a passing fancy to look at you, whilst in other cases the glance will be shot at you, suddenly and sharply, as if the party had been conscious of a mental call. The person obeying the call often will look embarrassed, and somewhat sheepish, when he meets your full magnetic gaze, which you have directed upon him when he turned his eyes in your direction.

Exercise 4. When talking with a person, and he seems to hesitate in the choice of a word, glance sharply at him and give a strong mental suggestion of a word. In many cases he will immediately repeat the word, which you have suggested. Your word must be appropriate, as otherwise his Passive mind may hesitate about using it, and his Active mind will step in and insert another word. Some students have tried this experiment in the case of a public speaker, preacher, etc., and have related many amusing instances in their experience. I remember reading a work, translated from a German writer, in which is mentioned the case of a youth whose powers of Concentration and Volation were most highly developed. He was a student at a leading college, and being more interested in athletic sports than in study, ran a great risk of falling behind in his work. Having discovered his powers, accidentally, he contrived a plan in the furtherance of which he would commit to memory but a few answers in each lesson. When the professor would start to quiz him he would send forth strong vibrations, willing the "professor" to select certain questions, the answer to which he had memorized, the result being that he stood up well in each class. The German writer, however, went on to say that his plan failed, the young man in his examination, as the final questions were being prepared by the faculty and submitted in writing, the student had no opportunity to try the "willing game" on the day of the examination.

Exercise 5. An interesting experiment is that of willing the movement of a person in a certain direction. This can be tried when walking behind a person on the street, by focusing the gaze as instructed. When the person approaches another person walking in the opposite direction, you may will the subject to turn either to the right or left, in passing the other person. You may also try this experiment in the case of a person approaching you in the street. In this case you should walk straight ahead, turning neither to the right nor to the left, keeping your gaze fixed on the approaching party, and making a mental command that he turn to the right or left, as you will.

Exercise 6. Stand at your window and fix your eyes upon an approaching person, at the same time willing that he turn his head and look at you whilst passing. You will find that he will obey your mental attraction, seven times out of ten, providing your powers of concentration are sufficiently well developed. Even without the practice of the Concentrations exercises, you will be able to influence passer by sufficiently often to satisfy you that there is "something in it." You will be able to obtain better results in this particular experiment, if you will stand at a first floor window rather than at a window higher from the ground. The motion of obeying the impulse and merely turning the head being so much easier than the motion of looking up to a second or third floor window, the percentage of results obtained by the first plan will greatly exceed those of the latter one. This exercise may be varied by the plan of compelling the attention of a person seated at a window, which you are passing, and so on. When you once begin to practice these exercises, you will find it so fascinating that you will invent new plans of testing your power, you being governed by the particular circumstances of the occasion.

These exercises will do much to develop confidence in your powers, and to aid you in acquiring the "knack" of sending out the vibratory impulses. They are of course more or less trifling in their natures, and unworthy of the exercise of the mental powers, except as a means of practice. They should not be used merely for the amusement of the student, and never for the amusement of his friends. One should never trifle with these mighty forces, nor exhibit them for the gratification of the vulgar curiosity of others. The student who grasps the real significance of the Law of Mental control will have little or no desire to parade his knowledge.

Chapter 10

TELEPATHIC VOLATION

Telepathy, an accepted fact—Wonderful progress of Psychic Science Thought transference—Vibrations—Wonderful proficiency of some—General knowledge not desirable—Danger of its use for improper purposes—Practical uses taught—General theory—How to obtain the best results—Advantages of concentration—Use of telepathic Volation prior to interview—To attract at a distance—How to obtain en rapport conditions—Full directions—Mental contact at a distance—Telepathic thought waves— Mental pictures—Moving circles of thought waves—The psychic tube—How to form and use it—Self-protection from the thought vibrations of others—Positive mental attitude—To shut out outside thought projections—How to prevent outside Pressure and influences—Effect of previous thought influences in personal interview—Matters rendered much easier—Proper mental attitude—Esoteric teaching for those prepared and qualified to receive it—Man findeth that which he seeketh—Diamonds or coal.

I will not attempt to take up your time in endeavoring to convince you of the existence of Telepathy. Psychic science has made such wonderful strides of late, that not only are its students fully aware of the truth of telepathy, but the general public as well are fully posted on the subject, and generally accept it as an established fact, as readily as they do the X Rays or Wireless Telegraphy. In fact, the public has always believed, in a general way, in thought transference, and the recent scientific experiments in telepathy have but served to confirm many people in their beliefs, which have been always entertained by them. The purpose of this lesson, therefore, is not to convince you of the fact that telepathy or thought transference is an existent fact, but to give you an idea of the proper means of using the same to your own advantage.

Every thought, whether voluntary or involuntary, causes thought waves or vibrations to be projected into space; with Vibrations, affect the minds of others to a greater or lesser degree.

There is a way to project thought vibrations toward another person, in a straight line, and thereby attract his attention to you. This plan, compared to the ordinary plan of undirected projection of thought waves, is as a rifle ball compared to a load of mustard seed shot. The rifle ball is vastly superior, providing you aim straight.

Some masters of mental science have attained a wonderful proficiency in the art of Telepathic Volation and some of the results secured by them would be deemed incredible by those not familiar with the laws of directed thought vibration. These results have been accomplished only by years of study, experiment, and the leading of a life far different from that of ordinary men. I fancy that very few of my readers would care to "pay the price" of such attainments.

It is well, perhaps, that this power is not easily acquired, as otherwise many might master it and use it for unworthy purposes. I am in the confidence of some of the masters of this wondrous power, and have witnessed many startling exhibitions of thought transference, but as the promise of secrecy was exacted from me by these friends, my lips are of course sealed. Outside of these-considerations, I would be of very doubtful wisdom to spread, broadcast information of this nature, which would place within the means of unscrupulous persons the power to work their wills upon their fellow men. Even as it is, fragments of this occult knowledge have leaked out and have been misused. Some have stumbled, by accident, upon some of the first principles, and hate pursued the matter as far as their limited knowledge would permit, often securing results which both surprised and startled them.

However, the purpose of this course of instruction is not to attempt to make its students venerable masters of occult lore, mystics, yogis, or wonder workers, but merely to give them a working knowledge of the laws of personal influence by means of the exercise of the powers of the mind—in short, Personal Magnetism. This being the case, I shall not dwell upon the wonderful phenomena produced at will by the masters of this science, but will proceed to give you an idea of the first principle sand practice of Telepathic Volation, which will be useful to you in your every day life. I shall not attempt to carry you further than the mere compelling the attention of the person whom you wish to influence, even if you have hundreds of miles removed from that person. If you wish to pursue the subject further, buy reading and experiment, you are at liberty to do so, but I warn you that you will find the attainment of the higher degrees of this science no easy task. The primary degrees, which I will now teach you, are quite easy of attainment, when the theory is once understood, and need only practice to make perfect.

As I have said before, all thoughts produce vibrations, which spread like ripples on a pond, produced by the casting in of a pebble. They affect people in all directions. If, however, you throw the pebble along the surface of the water, their ripples will manifest their energy in the direction in which the stone travels. So it is with the vibrations of telepathic volation, as compared with the vibrations of ordinary thought. For instance, suppose that you wish to attract the attention of any person whom you are desirous of interesting in your behalf. You may think earnestly of your desire to interest him, and if you have read something of Mental Science, you may picture him as being interested in you. By so doing, you will undoubtedly send forth strong thought vibrations in all directions, some of which will reach your man and may affect him to a greater or lesser degree, depending materially upon your degree of positive-ness toward him. At the best, he receives no stronger impulse than does any other person in any way connected with you. But, on the other hand, if you so arrange your mental telepathic apparatus that the strong vibratory impulse travels in a straight line to the desired person, the message will be received far more clearly. The impact of the vibrations will be much stronger.

In order to produce the best results, you should practice the exercise in the concentration given in this course. You will be able to produce some results without knowledge of Concentration, but with it you have ten-fold power. I will assume that you have acquired a working knowledge of Concentration, and have practiced the exercises. Now, for the production of results:

You expect to have an interview with a man, in a few days, in which you hope to interest him in your plans and enterprises. This man is perhaps a stranger to you, or at least is indifferent to you and there exists no attraction on his part towards you. You know that you will be able to in-fluence him by the methods already explained, but you wish, if possible, to open up direct communication with him before the interview—to get en rapport with him at a distance. You are perfectly right in feeling that your chances of success will be improved by these means, as once you manage to get en rapport with a man or woman, you have gained an important point, for that person cannot help feeling an interest in you thereafter—perhaps a strong interest.

The best plan for you to pursue, under the above circumstances, is to establish a mental rapport with your man by means of telepathic vola-tion. Your first step is to get by yourself, in some quiet place, and either lie down, or sit down in an easy chair. Get at ease, and relax every muscle; "let go" of your body until you are as limp as a damp cloth and are scarcely conscious of having a body. Calm yourself and secure a pas-sive, restful frame of mind, thinking of nothing outside of yourself, and, above everything else, shut out all disturbing fear thoughts. You will be able to do this easily by concentration.

After you have secured the proper condition, think intently, but calmly, of the other party. Do not frown or clinch your fists in your ef-forts to "think," but remain passive and relaxed—the effort must be a calm, steady mental effort. You will be assisted by the closing of the eyes and the production of a mental image of the person with whom you wish to get en rapport. If you have never seen this person, make the mental figure without distinct features. After a few trials you will notice that the mental picture seems more real to you, in fact, you realize that in some way you are in mental contact with the other person. When this stage is attained, then you will let your mind dwell on your wishes in re-gard to this person, and imagine him doing as you wish. Your principal mind picture, however, must be that of the man himself, as this holds the connection between you—the "day dreams" of his acting as you wish merely shaping the lesser thought waves. These lesser thought waves are, of course, moving in circles in all directions, but are reaching your man with much greater force than usual, the direct line of commu-nication being open. You will improve greatly by practice and experi-ment.

The best results are obtained when you get the impression of looking through a long tube about one foot in diameter, you being at one end and your man at the other. This impression, which can be acquired by concentration, is an indication of perfect rapport, and indicates that you have succeeded in shutting out all outside impressions and have opened up the psychic line of communication. When you attain this stage, you may rest assured that you are making a strong impression, unless the man at the other end of the psychic tube understands the law of mental control and had felt an indication of thought vibrations being directed toward him, in which case he will assume a "positive" mental state. The more passive the other man may be at that moment; the better will be the results. A little practice will develop this power, and you will get the impression of the "tube" more clearly, and will form a much clearer mental picture of the other person.

Some little practice may be required before you can obtain this mental impression of the long tube, although some students seem to be able to produce it fairly well at the first trial. You, of course will have secured the necessary passive condition in yourself. The next step is to produce the mental impression of the tubular connection. This will appear first as a faint, shadowy ring, which by degrees will become more distinct, and will resolve itself into the shape of an open end of a tube. The tube will then lengthen out, and, later on, you will be able to see clear along its enormous length. You may obtain this result in a few experiments, and, on the other hand, may be required to practice it a number of times. It seems to be greatly a matter of obtaining the "knack" of forming the mental picture. You may obtain good results without the production of the tubular effect, but the best results seem to be obtained by those who can produce this effect.

I may as well tell you at this point, that you should cultivate the "positive mental attitude," as it will enable you to obtain much better results and will prevent your being influenced by the exercise of Volation on the part of others. If you feel an indication of outside influence, you have merely to form the thought recognizing the "I AM" which will impart a feeling of psychical strength to you at once, and render you impervious to the vibrations. By a full appreciation and recognition of the higher self, you will surround yourself with a thought aura, which will protect you, without any voluntary effort of the mind from outside mental influences. Until you fully acquire this recognition you merely have to hold the thought for a moment, assert your real self by the affirmation "I AM," accompanied with the mental conception of the real self. A mental image of yourself surrounded by a protecting thought aura which deflects the vibrations of others, will, of itself, create an aura which deflects the vibrations of others, will, of itself, create an aura of moderate proportions which will last as long as you hold the thought, and will act as a perfect defense against outside vibrations. You should practice the production of these mental pictures, as the results will be of great value to you. If you ever feel that you wish to be alone and able to think without taking the opinions of others into consideration; just sit down and shut out the vibrations as above stated, and you will be surprised at the clearness of thought which will result. I will tell you in my next lesson about the influence of thought vibrations of others, even when not directed at us, move in widening circles, affecting us all more or less. Nature had provided us with instinctive powers of resistance, but nevertheless we are affected more or less by the thought vibrations of others, and what we think are our opinions are often merely the consensus of the opinions of others with whom we are surrounded. The change of residence by a man may result in his changing his views of religion, politics, ethics, etc., to correspond with the general impressions of his new environment, the change being wrought by the effect of the combined thought waves of his new neighbors. A little reflection will remind you of numerous instances of these phenomena: Waves of popular feeling will sweep over a country, arousing nearly every one, and then, will die out as suddenly as they came. A peaceable crowd may be converted into a savage mob, and so on; the emotions and opinions of a man being molded to a greater or lesser degree by the quality of the thought waves reaching him. You will readily see how valuable is the knowledge which will enable you to shut out these outside impressions at will, and allow you to be governed entirely by your own reason, judgment or intuition. Do not pass by this matter lightly, for the time may come when this knowledge will be of incalculable benefit to you. There are times in which clear thinking is of vital importance to every man. A powerful pressure may be brought on you to do a certain thing, and you are undecided just how to act. You need your best thought a this point, and the way to get it is to surround yourself with the protecting thought aura, and whilst secure in your own mental castle, decide what is best to be done. Many of your best decisions will be made in this way. By all means acquire the art.

I have digressed somewhat, in my desire to instruct you in the means of defense, and we will now resume our discussion of offensive methods. We will suppose that you have followed the instructions regarding the opening up of direct mental connections with your man by means of telepathic volation. When, later on, you come into his presence you will find that he seems to evince more interest in you than formerly; he will act as if he is better acquainted with you and has known you for years, and will consequently cause you to feel more "at home" with him that usual. I do not mean to say that he will, of necessity, do just what you have willed that he should (you have not advanced that far), but he will show a disposition to meet you half way, and matter will progress much more smoothly than might have been expected. Of course, a repetition of the exercise of telepathic volation will tend to "ease up" matters still more. Do not be discouraged at seeming failures, but keep at it and success will come when you least expect it.

In all interviews maintain a fearless, confident frame of mind, and do not forget to use the power of your eye. The latter often reopens the connection previously established by telepathic volation—reestablishes the rapport conditions—and makes the balance of the interview much more in conformity with your desires. You must be governed by circumstances and must learn to apply the above stated methods to widely differing conditions. The above sample is given you merely as an illustration. Its principles are correct and maybe apply, with appropriate variations, to any case in which you wish to influence another at a distance, preparatory to a personal interview. The principle is the same in all cases.

The student who has gone over these lessons carefully will discover much that will be missed by the casual reader. He will be able to read between the lines. If you are on the right track, much that has been stated will appear plainer to you with each reading. You will get new ideas every time you take up a lesson and read it, whilst the casual reader will merely skim over it and not enter into its spirit, the result being that such person will miss the esoteric teachings and will only see the outward or esoteric meaning, and will find the explanations and exercise about as "clear as mud." This is just as it is intended. Man findeth that which he seeketh. One man will find coal plainly exposed, whilst another will find the diamond embedded in the earth, but both diamond and coal are composed of the same material. "Ask and ye shall receive;" "seek and ye shall find." In concluding this lesson, let me say that whilst the powers of the mind, as illustrated in the forms set forth in this and preceding lessons, may appear wonderful, the power of thought as exemplified by what is known as the Adductive Power of Thought, far exceeds the phases of which I have told you. I will endeavor to impart to you an idea of this wonderful subject in our next lesson.

Chapter 11

THE ADDUCTIVE QUALITY OF THOUGHT

Prentice Mulford's theory—Thoughts are Things—Thought a dynamic force—Mind and matter identical—Miracles of Nature—Professor Gray's experiments with vibrations—Wonderful results—Professor Williams' significant statement—Food for thought—Character of thought vibrations—Murky thought waves and fleecy thought waves—Your thought retains a connection with you and affects you—Thought auras—Like attracts like A wonderful manifestation of psychic phenomena—Results of fear or worry thought—Advantage of confident thinking—Successful men the result of proper thought—Realized their ideal—Requisites for success—"I can and I will"—Others attracted toward you—Anything is yours if you only want it hard enough—Helen Wilman's theory.

That great writer on the power of the mind—Prentice Mulford, has summed up much of his philosophy in the statement: "Thoughts are Things." In these words he gave expression to a mighty truth, which, if fully apprehended by mankind, would revolutionize the world. Thought is not only a dynamic force, it is a real thing, just as is any other material object. Thought is merely a finer form of matter, or grosser form of spirit—you may call it either with equal correctness. Matter is but a grosser form of mind, mind but a finer form of matter. There is but one substance in nature, but that substance has many forms, ranging from the most material (so-called) forms, to the highest form—Spirit.

When we think, we send out vibrations of a fine ethereal substance, which is as real as the finer vapors or gasses, the liquids, the solids. We do not see thought—neither do we see the finer vapors or gasses. We cannot smell or taste thought—neither do we smell or taste the pure air. We can feel it however, as many can testify—which is more than we can say of the powerful magnetic vibrations of a mighty magnet, which, whilst exerting a force sufficient to attract toward it a piece of steel weighing a hundred pounds, is absolutely without effect upon us. Its vibrations may pass through our bodies and exert its force on the steel, while we may be unaware of its existence. Light and heat send out vibrations of a lower intensity than those of thought, but the principle is the same. The evidence of the five senses is not absolutely necessary to establish the existence of a material substance or force. The annuals of science are full of proofs of this fact, Professor Elisha Gray, and eminent scientist, says in his little book "The Miracles of Nature."

"There is much food for speculation in the thought that there exists sound waves that no human ear can hear, and color waves of light that no eye can see. The long, dark, soundless space between 40,000 and 400,000,000,000,000 vibrations per second, and the infinity of range beyond 700,000,000,000,000 vibrations per second, where light ceases, in the universe of motion, makes it possible to indulge in speculation."

M. M. Williams, in his work entitled "Short Chapters in Sciences," says, "There is no gradation between the most rapid undulations or tremblings that produce our sensation of sound, and the slowest of those which give rise to our sensations of gentlest warmth. There is a huge gap between them, wide enough to include another world of motion, all lying between our world of sound and our world of heat and light, and there is no good reason whatsoever for supposing that matter is incapable of such intermediate activity, or that such activity may not give rise to intermediate sensations, provided there are organs for taking up and sensifying these movements."

I cite the above authorities merely to give you food for thought, not to attempt to demonstrate to you the fact that thought vibrations exist. The last mentioned subject would be far beyond the scope and purposes of this work, and can only be touched upon herein.

The character of the thought vibrations sent out by us depends upon the nature of the thought itself. If thought had color (and some say that they have), we should see our fear and worry thought as murky, heavy, clouds hanging close to the earth; our bright, cheerful and happy, confident, "I can and I will' thought as light, fleecy, vapory clouds hanging close to the earth; our bright, cheerful and happy, confident, "I can and I Will" thoughts as light, fleecy, vapory clouds, traveling swiftly and mingling with others of their kind, forming fleecy cloud banks, high above the level of the dense, mephitic, foul exhalations produced by fear and worry "I can't" thoughts.

No matter how far your thought waves may travel, they retain a certain connection with you and exert an influence over you as well as others. You cannot easily get rid of the influence over you as well as others. You cannot easily get rid of the influence of these "children of your mind." If you have been sending out bad thoughts, you are subject to their influence, and your only hope is to neutralize and counteract them by sending out strong, new thought waves of the proper sort, or by asserting the I AM, and thereby creating a mental aura, or by both means.

The old saying "Like attracts like" and "Birds of a feather flock together," are both literally exemplified by the tendencies of thought waves. There is what is known as the "Adductive Quality of Thought," the word "adductive" being derived from the Latin word *adductum*, to bring to. The manifestation of this quality of thought is one of the most wonderful features in the realm of psychic phenomena.

Fear or worry thought will attract others of their own kind, and will combine with them, the result being that you will be afflicted not only by the product of your own mind, but also by those emanating from the minds of others, the whole forming a heavy burden. And the longer that you persist in that line of thought, the heavier will be your burden. On the other hand, if you think bright, cheerful and happy thoughts they will draw to themselves others of the same degree, and you will feel brighter, more cheerful and happier from their combined influence. This is absolutely true, but you are not asked to accept it on faith alone. Try it and be convinced. But, in the experiment, be sure to couple the thoughts with a feeling of confidence in the outcome, and you will obtain much better and quicker results. Half-hearted, doubting thoughts have only a small percentage of the force of confident, expectant ones.

If you think along the lines of discouragement, lack of confidence, "afraid to try," "know I can't" lines, you will attract to yourself the force of other murky thoughts of the same kind, and you will find that you really "can't," and moreover, everyone else will seem to entertain just the same opinion regarding your ability. But just brace up and send out earnest, confident, fearless, "I can and I WILL" thought waves, and you will attract to yourself the similar thought waves of others, which will still further stimulate and strengthen you, and help you to accomplish your aims.

If you send out jealous, envious thoughts, they will come home bringing their mates with them, and you will be wretched until the effect passes off. So will waves of hate return to harm you, having gained force and power on their journey. The old proverb "Curses like chickens come home to roost," is much nearer the real truth than is generally supposed. Anger thought arouses anger in the other man (unless he has rendered himself positive to them), and he sends back his return thought waves; besides which other anger waves mingle and help on the vicious work. You have heard people say, "A man always finds what he looks for." Of course he does, he cannot help it, for his thought attracts others of the same sort, and he sees a world of the same color as his mental spectacles.

Good thought attracts good—evil thoughts, evil. If you hate a man and send him your hate thoughts, you will get hate in return, and will face a hating and hateful world. In the thought world, you get back what you send out—with good interest. Send out kind thoughts and kind thoughts will return to you, with compound interest, and you will find yourself greeted by a kind, helping world, and will be much the gainer. If only from a selfish point of view, it pays to think the best thoughts. If you will practice thinking along these lines for, say, one month, you will find the greatest difference in things, the greatest change in yourself, and you will find that you look with aversions and disgust upon your old, mean, low, miserable way of thinking, and would not return to it under any consideration—no, not for a fortune. Before the month will have passed you will be conscious of the helpful force of the responsive thought waves, and your life will seem entirely different to you. Try it. Try it now. You will never regret it.

There are two particularly bad thoughts, which you should root out, first of all, and you will find that, when you have rid yourself of the balance will die out of their own accord. I allude to Fear and Hate. These two following weeds are the parents of most of the others. Worry is the oldest child of Fear, and bears a close resemblance to its father. Envy, Malice, and Anger are some of the numerous broods claiming Hate as their parent. Destroy the "old ones" and you will not be troubled with their offspring. I will speak further on this point in the lesson on Character Building.

I will now process to another phase of the Adductive Quality of Thought. I refer to its exhibition along the lines of Success by right Thinking.

It may seem almost incredible to you, but it is a fact, that all successful men owe their greatness to their earnest, forceful, concentrated thought vibrations. They fixed their mind upon a certain line of thought; brought the aid of Will—the recognition of the I AM—to bear on that line of thought; allowed that line of thought to mold their characters; went straight to the mark at which they and aimed in the beginning. Others had aimed for the same mark, but failed because they failed to hold the thought, and had allowed themselves to become discouraged, intimidated, tempted or coaxed away form their ideal.

The requisites for the successful follow-up of a thought ideal to the end, are, first, an overpowering Desire (not a mere wish); second, a strong belief in your ability to accomplish your desire (not a mere half-hearted faith); and, third, an invincible Determination to win (not a mere back boneless—"I'll try to").

It is a strange thing and difficult to explain (without leading you into metaphysical depths), but the measure of success by this plan seems to depend materially upon your belief in the force. A half-hearted belief will bring only half-way results, whilst an earnest, firm, confident belief that "your win will come to you" will accomplish results little short of marvelous. Cultivate that sort of belief, and accompany it with a firm mental demand for what you want, and you will succeed. "Ask and you shall receive, knock and it shall be opened unto you," but accompany the asking and knocking with the firm belief and expectation of Success.

Helen Wilman says:

"He who dares assert the I
May calmly wait

While hurry fate
Meets his demand with sure supply."

But the words "calmly wait" refer only to the state of mind—and indicates that calm, confident expectation of a "sure thing." It does not mean that a man shall sit down and fold his hands and do nothing more than "calmly wait" for "hurrying fat" to drop his reward in his lap. Oh, no. Helen Wilmans never meant that—she is not built that way. The man, who is possessed of the dominating desire, and concentrated thought impulses, does not sit down and merely wait—he couldn't do that without sacrificing his keen desire and earnest pursuit. "Thought manifests itself in Action"—the firmer the thought, the stronger the action. You may want a thing in the worst way, and be fully confident of your ability to secure it, but you are going after that thing the best way you know how, and are "going to get it." You will agree with Garfield, who said, "Do not wait for a thing to turn up—go out and turn something up," with all your might and main, but carrying with you the calm demand that that thing will be "turned up as the result of your going out and turning." And you will feel all the time the confident expectation of the "thing" obeying your command.

I wish that my space would allow me to tell you of the wonderful results of this plan of thinking and acting, but I can merely touch upon it and call your attention to the workings of the Law. But, after all, one must learn a thing by experience before they will appreciate its truth. The I AM is not satisfied in any other way. I want everyone who reads this lesson to start in and practice the New Thought plan. You will have to accept what I say on faith, at first, but you will soon begin to demonstrate its correctness by personal experience, and then you will know it to be true, and will push forward toward Success.

Anything is yours, if you only want it hard enough. Just think of it. Anything. Try it. Try it in earnest and you will succeed. It is the operation of a mighty Law.

Our next lesson will take up the subject of Character Building, and will show you that "as a man thinketh in his heart, so is he."

Chapter 12

CHARACTER BUILDING BY MENTAL CONTROL

Man can make of himself what he will—Regeneration no idle dream—A living truth— Strong faculties made stronger, weak faculties developed—The new "Regenerator"—The Law of Mental Control—The new path through the woods—Making yourself over—To break up old thought habits and form new ones—The four great methods—Force of Will—Hypnotic Suggestion—Auto Suggestion—Thought Absorption—Ideal treatment—Full instruction in the theory of each of the four methods, showing their respective advantages and disadvantages, with illustrations of each—How to acquire a desired quality of mind—The practice of Thought Absorption—Practical exercises and directions—Exercises 1 to 6—You are your own master—Make of yourself what you will.

The student who has read the preceding lessons has doubtlessly said, after reading some of the statements contained therein, "Yes, that is all true enough, and I could accomplish these results if I but possessed the necessary qualities of mind and character."

This seems to be the great stumbling block to many. They know just what is necessary to produce Success, but because they do not possess the characteristics of the successful man they fancy, that the prize is beyond their reach. There is no greater mistake in the work that this false belief, this kind of fear thought, this lack of recognition of the power of the I AM.

Man can so mold his mind by the power of the will that can make of himself practically what he will. He can "make over" himself, without a doubt. A man is just what he wills himself to be. This is a bold statement, but it is absolutely true and we have hundreds of instances of it in every city in this land. Hundreds of men can testify to its correctness, and many hundreds of others are on the road. Regeneration is no idle dream. It is a living truth. You will realize just what this means, if you will stop to consider that every effect has its cause. Business success is due to certain qualities of mind, character or temperament. Of these three qualities, the first is the only real one, as the last two are but the results of the first. Those who have the given qualities, produce the given result; those lacking the said qualities, fail to obtain the result. When once you realize that these qualities are within your grasp—that you can make them a part of yourself, you will readily see that wonderful possibilities are open to you. The acquirement of these qualities is key to the situation.

You know just what these necessary qualities are: Energy, Ambition, Determination, Courage, Confidence, Perseverance, Patience, Prudence, and the rest of the list.

All persons possess some of these qualities, and lack others. Some are strong in some of these qualities, and weak in others. And every man instinctively knows in just what respect he falls short. He may not admit it to his friends, or even to his wife, but deep down in his inner consciousness lurks the knowledge of the truth. If he could acquire the missing qualities by a mere wish, he would know just what to wish for. No doubt about that.

But he lacks the confidence and perseverance thought to be necessary for the acquirement of that which he knows he needs. He is not willing to pay the price of attainment. If some great scientist would announce to the world that he had discovered some wonderful chemical combination, or some new "serum," that would develop the shrunken and atrophied faculties of the mind, and which would render a man stronger in the qualities wherein he had been weak, what a rush there would be for the new "regenerator." Thousands would want it, and every man would be able to tell just what brand of serum he needed. He would need the diagnosis or prescription for that. Every man would be able to diagnose his own case and order the serum indicated by his symptom. One would want triple extract of Energy; another, the "Stick-to-it" brand; another, the vial bearing the confident *"I Can"* label; and so on. They would be able to round out their characters, and command success. Now, there is no drug that will produce this result. And there never will be. But the desired result can be obtained by the operation of the law of Mental Control.

I can give you but a general idea of the workings of this great law, but if you will pay attention to what I have to say on the subject, you will grasp the principle, and will be able to work out your own salvation. The first point to remember is that we are all creatures of habit, bodily and mentally. Our characteristics are largely the result of habits of thought. We may have inherited impulses which made it easier to form certain habits, and more difficult to form certain habits of thought, and more difficult to form others, and we consequently move along the lines of the least resistance; but the character is, after all, the result of certain acquired habits. We follow well worn mental paths, in preference to making new paths through the woods, even though we know that the new path would be the better, by far, and that is would be as easy to travel over as the present one, when it was finally formed. We know all this. It is an old story. Then why do we not start in to make the new path? Simply because "it is too much trouble." We lack the will power, determination and persistency to do it. I admit that it is no easy task, but think of the reward.

These things are "ancient history" to you, of course, but I have something else to say to you on the subject that is not so "antiquated." I propose to make you a present of a labor saving "path maker," which is guaranteed to clear away the underbrush and rubbish in but a fraction of the time, and with much less labor, that the old plodding clearing away process.

This new plan is very simple, but very effective, and will enable you to "make yourself over" without the ripping apart process dependent upon the other method. I will tell you about it in as few words as possible. I have already explained to you that your mind possess two planes of effort, two functions, the Active and the Passive. The Active function does the volitional, original thinking, whilst the Passive function does only what it is told to do by the Active function (or by others). The Passive function is the easygoing partner of the firm, to whom I introduced you in a previous lesson. It is this part of the mind upon which hypnotists operate, after lulling to sleep the Active function, the critical partner. The Passive function, although in a sense the inferior, really rules us, unless we know how to manage it. It is the habit-function, the beaten-track function, of whose existence we are all conscious. It is easily influenced, but nevertheless is "set" in its ways. Tell it a thing over and over—something, which you wish it to believe—and it will end up accepting the new thought and being as "set" in the new notion as it was in the former one. This is the secret of breaking up the habits of thought; action; disposition; and character. The suggestion upon which the Passive function acts may come from your own Active mind, or from the mind of another. This is the explanation of the beginning of a habit, good or bad. To break up old thought habits, and to replace them with new habits of thinking, one or more of several plans may be used. One may accomplish the results by sheer force of will; another by hypnotic suggestion from an experienced qualified operator; to your Passive mind, a fourth by that which I will term Thought Absorption. Breaking up thought-habits by sheer force of will is a most difficult task, as most of us know, for we have all tired it. It is a plan by which only the strongest succeed whilst the weaker are defeated and relinquish the effort, experiencing additional discouragement and despair. We accomplish this result by the "strengthening of the will," or more correctly by the strengthening of the Active Function of the mind by the will, enabling it to step in and simply command the Passive function to drop the old thought-habit and adopt the new in its place. It is a magnificent feat, but very difficult of performance. The same result can be obtained by an easier plan. The very habit of making the Passive mind more amendable to the commands of the Active function can be acquired by the easier plan of which I will speak in this lesson.

The second plan, the changing of the thought-habit by Hypnotic Suggestion, has been followed by many, with excellent results, provided, always, that the operator was a proper person, thoroughly understanding his profession, and being fully acquainted with the latest methods of eradicating undesirable thought-habits. In this connection, I would say that one should be very careful in whose hands they place themselves for treatment of this sort. One should not trust their case to a person just because that person could give hypnotic suggestion; one would not employ a man as cashier of a bank just because the applicant could keep books, and count money rapidly.

The third plan, which of producing the result by autosuggestion is good, especially when accompanied by Thought Absorption. In auto-suggestion you simply keep on repeating to the Passive mind the state-ment that the new habits exist (ignoring the old one), and the Passive mind, although inclined to be a little rebellious at first, will eventually accept what you say as thought. It will adopt the new thought-habit as its own thought just as do some people under like circumstances. Auto-suggestion is practically self-hypnosis of the passive mind by the Active mind. It is a case of "every man his own hypnotist."

The third plan, taught Absorption, consists in the placing of yourself in a perfectly passive condition, at frequent intervals and fixing the mind intently upon the idea or mental statement, that the new habits exist; picturing yourself, by an effort of the imagination, as being a man pos-sessed to the desired qualities. You should "carry the thought" with you continually, picturing yourself as possessing the desired habit, in every leisure moment, day and night, an din other ways acting out the belief. This is purely an action of the Passive mind, assisted by the imagination. It seems very simple, but the results, which have been attained by it, seem little short of marvelous. It is by far the easiest, and one of the most effective methods of making over your character. The imagined thing becomes a reality in a comparatively short time, and action follow close upon he heels of thought.

In my opinion the combination of autosuggestion and Thought Ab-sorption afford the ideal treatment in Character Building. If persisted in, it will accomplish the most marked results in a comparatively shore space of time, the effect being felt from the very first. Do not pass over this lightly; because it seems so simple. It is a secret worth thousands of dollars to you, and one, which you would not part with for any money, once you have experienced its benefits.

I will now give you a brief explanation of the several methods above referred to. Let us take the Fear (worry) thought-habit, as an illustration. It affords an excellent illustration of the bad habits of the rest of the bad thought, for it does more to unfit one for the duties of life than all the rest of the bad thoughts combined, and also brings with it the vile brood of miserable weakening thought-habits of which it is the parent. The man who has torn out by the roots the vile Fear thought (worry thought) has progressed a long distance on the road to Freedom. Fear thought never helped anyone, and never will; but it has wrecked the careers of thousands of men and women, paralyzing their energies, preventing their progress, enfeebling their minds, and diseasing their bodies. We have all felt it, and those of us who have banished it would not return to its thralldom under any consideration. Life is an entirely different thing to the man who has rooted out this noxious weed. He becomes an entirely different order of being. Most of the things we fear never occur; and the few that do occur can be rooted by a bold front, aided by the strength, which the absence of Fear and Worry imparts. The energy and vital force wasted on Worry is more that sufficient to enable us to conquer our real troubles when they occur. You remember the tale of the old man on his deathbed, giving his son good advice, who said: "John, I have lived eighty years and have had many troubles, the majority of which never occurred." The old man merely voiced the experience of all men or women who have lived to old age. The moral is obvious.

I will suppose that you are a victim to Fear thought (and I am very likely correct) and that you are about to try the four plans of ridding yourself of it. I will suppose that you will try them in turn one after the other. You will first try the power of the Will, and will say to yourself: "I will not Fear," "I command Fear to depart." This is the heroic remedy. I shall not go into details of this treatment. You know all about it, already. You have all tried it. You will next try the effect of Hypnotic Suggestion, and will employ a good suggestionist who will place you in an easy position; cause you to relax every muscle; quiet every nerve and assume a state of mental calm; and who, having secured your undivided, concentrated attention, will give you strong, repeated suggestions of Fearlessness, Courage, Hopefulness, Confidence, etc. The capable suggestionist will study each case closely, and by carefully selected, and properly administered suggestions, will plant the seed of the new thought-habit with its designed to supplant and crowd out the old one. Splendid results are obtained by this line of treatment. The writer has cured many persons of undesirable thought-habits in this way, when they felt that they preferred outside help. He has also used this form of treatment in order to get the patient started on the right mental path; to give him confidence in himself and in the efficacy of this form of mental development; and then instructed him in the theory and practice of auto-suggestion and Thought Absorption, leaving him to finish the fight himself. You will then try the power of autosuggestion by constantly repeating to yourself the words: "I am Fearless"; "I am Confident"; "I have abolished Fear"; "I Fear Nothing," etc. These autosuggestions must be made earnestly, just as if you were suggesting to another person, and you must endeavor to live up to them.

Let your Passive mind see—that you believe what you say, and it will have confidence in your statements, and, accepting them as correct, will act accordingly. If you go about this practice in good faith and in earnest, you will notice an improvement from the first. You must remember, however, that if the Passive mind thrusts a Worry thought upon your consciousness, you must double your assertion of Fearlessness, until the intruder retreats. This may bother you at the first, for the Worry thought is pretty confident of a friendly reception, but like any other mangy cur it will soon learn that you carry a club, and will bear a hasty retreat at the mere sight of it.

Carry this idea of the cur and the club in your mind, and you will have but little trouble with the brute. You will learn to despise the Worry thought as you do the snarling, snapping cur, and will not hesitate to deal him a good sound whack with your mental club, provided he stays long enough to be hit. He will soon retreat with his tail between his legs, and will thereafter manifest a wholesome respect for the club. Don't wait until he actually bothers you, but get in the habit of reaching out for the club at the first sight of the yellow hide of the mongrel.

And now you are ready to try the effects of Thought absorption. In this case you place yourself in the suggestible, passive condition, just as you did at the bidding of the suggestionist when was preparing to give you helpful suggestions. The more passive you become, the better will be the effect. In other words, you relax, let go, and become perfectly passive, bodily and mentally. You thus relieve the Active mind from duty and allow the Passive mind to have undisputed control. You then carry the thought of "I am Fearless," and the others above given, calmly and firmly. You also picture yourself, on your imagination, as being Fearless, acting fearlessly, having moral and physical courage, and as driving away the Worry mongrel with our mental club.

Give your imagination full scope, but hold it down to the desired line of thought. You will find the exercises in concentration most valuable here. You also will carry the thought of Fearlessness with you all the time, and endeavor to act the part naturally. I mean adjust what I say; act the part just as does the actor when he assumes a role. The assumed character will soon become more real, and in time will be the "real thing" with you. After a little practice, it will become second nature to you; and eventually will become your real nature.

As I have said before, the combination of Thought Absorption and Autosuggestion forms the ideal treatment in Character Building. I will close this lesson with a few exercises designed to aid you in Thought Absorption. Do not forget to practice the Concentration exercises, but do not wait to master them before commencing your fight on the Fear thought cur. Commence this flight at once. Cut your club today, and just "lay" for the brute. Once you get him out of the way, you will be able to pursue the study of this subject, without the annoyance of having him around, howling and yelping at you. The treatment for lack of Energy, Confidence, Perseverance, etc., is identical with that directed for Fear thought, the words of the auto-suggestions and affirmations, of course, being, altered to suit the particular case.

The Practice of Thought Absorption

1. Find a secure, quiet place, as far as possible removed from the scenes and sounds of the outside world. If the ideal conditions cannot be secured, you must content yourself with the best obtainable conditions. The idea is to shut out the distracting, impression, and enable you to be alone with yourself.

2. Place yourself on a couch, bed or easy chair, obtaining a position of absolute ease and comfort. Relax every muscle; withdraw the tension from every nerve; allow yourself to be perfectly "limp" all over, from head to feet. Breathe deeply and slowly, retaining the breath for several moments before expelling it; continue the deep breathing until a feeling of calm, restful quiet manifests itself.

3. Concentrate your whole attention inwardly upon yourself, shutting out all outside impressions. Concentration exercises will enable you to do this.

4. Having obtained the proper conditions of bodily and mental relaxation, fix your thought firmly, calmly and steadily upon the word "*fearless,*" letting its outward form sink into your mind, as they dive into the wax. Give yourself up to the thought and the word. Then think of the meaning of the word, the characteristics of a person possessing that, quality, etc.

5. Form the mental picture of yourself possessed of the desired quality, act it out in your mind, as in a dream; think of yourself doing certain things by reason of the possession of the woman, you being possessed of the desired quality. In short, indulge in a pleasant "day dream," having for its theme your possession of the quality desired. Give your imagination full sway, merely insisting upon it sticking to the text, and it's always showing you successful the scenes and occurrences of the dream. Always conclude this "dream" with a strong impression and thought of "I AM."

6. Repeat these exercises as often as possible. It is like the dripping of the water on the stone. The repeated thought takes root and grows rapidly. It is a good plan to practice this exercise when you retire for the night, and also during your waking hours at night, if you have any. The exercises will not keep you from slumber, but will rather tend to induce the desire for sleep. If you feel yourself dropping into a doze, do not resist it, as the impression, which you carry with you into sleep, will dwell with you, and will do its work even while you are slumbering.

In the above exercises, I have used the word "Fearless" and its accompanying thought, to illustrate the process of inducing Thought Absorption. You will understand that you are to use the word expressing the quality of which you are desirous of acquiring. If you wish to rid yourself of an undesirable quality, select the word expressing the opposite thought. For instance, if you are inclined to be indolent, select the word "Active" or "Energy," etc., and so on. You must remember that when we wish to brighten a room, we do not have to drive out the darkness first; we merely open the blinds and admit the light, and lo, the darkness has departed. Do not bother about the undesirable thought, but concentrate on their opposites, and the positive will neutralize the negative. Do not become discouraged if the results do not come as soon as you would like. Remember, they are sure to come, in time. All that you require is repeated practice. The mind can be developed just as can be the muscles, and by the same process—continued practice.

You have been given the means of remedying your defects. If you do not avail yourself of its benefits, it is simply because you do not want to. If you have Desire strong within you, you will do it. If you lack the strong desire, I cannot help you. If you prefer to sell your glorious birthright of Mental Control for the mess of pottage of present indulgence, that is your own business. You are your own master. Make of yourself what you will.

Chapter 13

The Art of Concentering

*Definition of the term—Exoteric and esoteric meanings—A valuable acquirement—
Thought combined with action—Volitional concentering—How to "arrive"—
Advantages of concentering—Means of doing the best work—Getting the full result of
your work—Cure for discouragement—Work out your own salvation—Don't be a
human doormat—Get down to business—Heaven's not a loafing place—Work robbed of
its terrors—Remedy for the "blues"—A specific for discouragement—Concentering no
easy task—A simple experiment—Advantages of concentering—No more waste effort or
lost motion—Focusing the attention—Focusing thought—A valuable remedy for mental
and physical exhaustion—Explanation—Requisites of concentering.*

In ordinary conversation, we make frequent use of the word "Concentration," in the sense of "bringing together," or "diminishing in bulk and increasing in strength," or "consolidating," etc. In order to avoid an erroneous conception, I have preferred to use the term "Concentering." A plain definition of the word "Concentering" is "the bringing to a common center," or "focusing." Carry in your mind the analysis of the word, thus "Con-*center*,"—"to bring to a center."

The word "concenter" has its exoteric, or common meaning, and its esoteric, or hidden, meaning, when used in connection with the exercise of the powers of the mind. The exoteric idea is the concentering of the mind upon the one particular thought or action, inhibiting all outside thoughts or impressions. The esoteric idea is the concentering of the mind upon the Ego, the I AM, inhibiting all outside thoughts or impressions. The esoteric idea is the concentering of the mind upon the Ego, the I AM, inhibiting all thoughts of the material body or of the grosser self, and dwelling the higher regions of the Soul. The First mentioned form of concentering is a most valuable acquirement for man in his everyday life; the second form is a most desirable acquirement for those who would know more of their real self, and who aspire to know something of the secrets of *the silence*. In this lesson I will speak exclusively of the practical side of concentering, that being the purpose of this work. I have, however, given the reader hints of the esoteric phase, that he may know how to proceed if he is attracted to the same.

The art of concentering upon a give thought or action is one of the most desirable acquirements, which a man can possess. We have been told the advantage of "doing a thing with all our might," and "doing one at a time, and doing it well," etc. We all know of the painter who attributed his excellent work to the fact that he "mixed brains in his painting," and of the miner who "put a little brains into his pick."

We know that the simplest task is better performed, if we but combine concentered thought with the action. Workmen differ in degree according to the amount of concentered thought placed in their work. The man who "takes an interest in his work," and who finds an intellectual pleasure in his daily task, is the man who does the best work, and is also the happier man. The man who keeps his eye on the clock, or who "leaves his pick in the air at the sound of the whistle," is a mere machine, and will never amount to anything, unless he changes his point of view regarding work. The man who "thinks with his hands," or who can "carry a message to Garcia," is in demand. He is a scarce article, and many employers are looking for him. When will our boys learn to appreciate this fact?

Well, what has all this to do with Concentering? Just this, that the interest and brains that a man puts into his work is the result of an exercise of volitional concentering. The man who practices concentering in his daily life, shuts out distracting impressions, and gives his best thought force to the task before him, and does better work by reason thereof, whether he be day laborer, architect, clerk, salesman, poet, painter or banker. Every man who has "arrived" has developed the art of concentering. He may not realize it, but he has, just the same. And more, any man who will develop the art of concentering will "arrive." Try it and be convinced. Why, you can see it for yourself; it cannot help producing the result. If you concenter on an object, and hold the thought firmly, you cannot help doing the best work, and if you do the best work you will receive the proper reward, providing you have the sense with which you were born, and have not allowed yourself to be hypnotized into a belief that you are a worm of the dust, or a human doormat. If you do the best work, you will find a market for your services; if your present employer doesn't appreciate you, there are plenty of others who will. But you will have to do the work—don't forget that. No man is going to be fool enough to pay you for something that you do not do. Oh, no, he is not built that way, and he would not "arrive" if he did. But, just the same, he will not permit you to leave his employ for that of his rival, if you do the best work, and you will do the best work if you only will get down to business, and concenter. If you have been discouraged by your apparent lack of success in your vocation, just you learn how to concenter and do it; spit on your hands and take a fresh grip, a little high up, and pull for all you're worth. You just pull hard enough, and something will be sure to give at the other end of the rope. Don't you waste your time complaining of the "oppression of Capital" and all that sort of thing. If you are a "concentering" man, Capital will soon fall all over itself to secure your services, or to buy your goods. Can't you see it, man? Of course you do. Well, then, stop fooling around about it, and get to work in earnest. Get a move on, and hustle. If you refuse to accept the means of financial salvations now offered you, why just lie around and be a human doormat all your life; who cares! If a man is too lazy to be saved, why, just let him be—the other thing. It serves him right. Some of you fellows need a man around you with a spiked club, with instructions to give you a good bang every time you slack up and engage in mental wool-gathering. Stop your "moaning" and get down to business. Some people spend their life in dreaming of the hereafter, where they expect to spend their time "loafing around the throne." Now, they're sure to be fooled about that. All Nature is in motion, and God is working hard every day, and I believe that when you get to the other shore you will be confronted with a sign having thereon inscribed the words, *"No Loafing Permitted."* If you take an interest in your work, you rob it of its terrors. Start in, man, and work out your own salvation from poverty and unhappiness. Do it, and do it *now*.

The man who can concenter has at his hand a sure remedy for the "blues." How? Why, just by shutting off the unpleasant thought and concentering on a brighter subject. Now, don't say that you can't do this. You can do it, if you acquire the "knack." Thousands of people have found this plan a specific for the "blues," discouragement, worry, fear, and the rest. Try it, and you will find that life will appear entirely different to you. Try it, and you will feel so good that you would not call the President your cousin. Try it, and you will "feel the thrill of life along your keel," and will thank God that you are alive, instead of curing the day when you were born. You will do your work better; you will feel better; you will be better. Is it not worth the trial?

You may have an idea that you know something about concentering. Well, maybe you do; let's see. Take up a lead pencil and try to sharpen it properly. Take your time at it, and turn out a first class job. Now, see if you can concenter on that pencil sharpening, to the exclusion of all outside thoughts; try to devote your best energy and thought to the task at hand. For the moment, live for the sole purpose of getting an A-1 point on that pencil.

Well, how did it feel? Pretty hard job, wasn't it? Yes, I thought so. You need practice young man. Take up the exercises given in this lesson, and go over them until you can do anything, whatsoever, without your thoughts wandering. Anyone can concenter upon an agreeable task, but just give them an unpleasant or monotonous, job, and you will find that their thought will wander away in spite of them; that is, until they learn to concenter by an effort of the will. That is the test—the ability to concenter upon an unpleasant, unattractive, monotonous task. When you have overcome these troubles, you will know that you have broken the backbone of Waste Effort of Lost Motion. By concentering you are able to focus your attention, thought and energy upon a given thing, thereby obtaining the best possible results. The rays of the sun, when focused upon an object by means of a sunglass, produce a heat many time greater that the direct relay of the same source of light and heat. So it is with that attention. Scatter it and you get but ordinary results; but focus it upon the thing to be done, and you obtain a wonderful amount of energy. The concentering man focuses his attention, and thought force, upon an object, and the result is that his every action, voluntary and involuntary, is in the direction of the attainment of that object. As I said in a previous lesson, a man can have everything he wants if only he wants it hard enough. If his energies are focused upon a thing, to the exclusion of everything else, the force so generated and focused must bring the result.

The moral of all this is: "Whatsoever you do, do it with all your might." Do it in earnest. "Do one thing at a time, and do it well."

In order to obtain the best results from the thought-coerces, as explained in preceding lesson, you should acquire the art of concentering. By focusing the thought, you add to its strength, as a moment's reflection will show you. The exercises accompanying the preceding lessons should be accompanied by the exercises in concentering. These exercises are more or less tedious and monotonous, but should be persisted at until perfected. You will be repaid for your work by the conscious increase in your powers of concentering, which will be apparent from the first.

There is one thing more that I wish to say to you, before starting in with the exercises, and that is to point out to you the advantage of concentering, as a means of mental and physical rest. If this were the only result obtainable by the exercises, it would be worth your while to acquire it. Suppose you feel completely tired out by some physical or mental labor, and are sadly in need of rest. If you lie down, the thought, which has been occupying your mind, returns to haunt you, and prevents your mind from obtaining the much-needed rest. Now, the theory is that each thought calls into operation and activates certain sets of brain cells—the other cells of course taking a rest in the meantime. This being the case, you will see, readily, that when one set of brain cells become utterly fagged out by excessive exercises and work, its only chance of getting an entire rest is for you to concenter upon an entirely different line of thought, shutting out the cells which you have just tired out, and which are still vibrating with excitement from the strong impetus given them. By concentering upon the new thought, the old cells are relieved from further work and obtain a much-needed rest. These cells are hungry for work, and may attempt to return to their task in spite of you, but if you have acquired proficiency in the art of concentering, you have learned to master them. You doubtless remember the time when your brain felt exhausted by the hard work of the business day, but when you pickup up an interesting novel you became so interested in it that your old brain cells "knocked off" for a while, and when the novel was completed you felt completely refreshed, not withstanding the fact that the reading of the book was in itself no slight exercises of the mind. That is the theory. Now, put it into practice, and you will have no need to complain of mental overwork. You will be able to put thoughts off and on, like your coat, changing them whenever you see fit.

I will now give you a few exercises, the practice of which will enable you to develop the power of concentering. In leaving this phase of the subject, I again would remind you that the underlying principle of concentering is the focusing of the attention upon a certain thought or action. Any exercise, which will strengthen the faculty of volitional inhibition of non-essential thought, will be of value, the exercises herein given here being merely furnished as suggestions of others.

Chapter 14

THE PRACTICE OF CONCENTERING

Exercises in the concentering—Shutting out outside impressions—Conquering inattention—Cultivating will power—Training the body to obey the will—Volitional control of muscular movements—Not so easy of acquirements—Sitting still exercises—Controlling muscles of the arm—Exercises—Steadying the muscles—Exercises—Cultivate equanimity and mental and physical ease—Examples-Getting rid of ugly habits of motion—Volitional attention—Exercises developing same—Direction for additional exercise—Concentered attention upon outside object—General explanation—Miscellaneous exercises.

The fist requisite of concentering is the ability to shut out outside thoughts, sounds and sights; to conquer inattention; to obtain perfect control over the body and mind. The body must be brought under the direct control of the mind; the mind under the direct control of the will. The Will is strong enough, but the Mind needs strengthening by being brought under the direct influence of the Will. The Mind, strengthened by the impulse of the Will, becomes a much more powerful projector of thought vibrations, than otherwise, and the vibrations have much greater force and effect.

In these exercises I will begin with training the body to readily obey the commands of the Mind.

The first exercise, and one which must be mastered before the succeeding exercises are undertaken, is the control of the muscular movements. This, at first sight, may appear very simple, but a few experiments will convince you that you have much to learn. The following exercises will be of great benefit to you in acquiring perfect control of the muscles.

1. Sit still. This is no easy task. It will at first try your powers of concentering, to refrain from involuntary muscular movements, but by a little practice you will be able to sit still, without a movement of the muscles, for fifteen minutes or more. The best plan is to place yourself in an easy chair, assuming a comfortable position, then relax all over, and endeavor to remain perfectly quiescent for a period of five minutes. Continue this exercise until you can accomplish it with ease, and then increase the time to ten minutes. After you have mastered the ten minutes exercise, increase the time to fifteen minutes, which is about as far as you need pursue the exercises. You should not tire yourself with this, or any of our other exercises. The better plan is to practice a little at a time, but as often as possible. Bear in mind that you must not sit in a rigid position; there must be no strain on the muscles; you must relax completely. This plan of relaxing will prove valuable to you when you wish to get a good rest after fatiguing physical exertion. It is an ideal "rest cure," and may be taken either sitting in a chair or lying down on a couch or bed.

2. Sit erect in your chair, with your head up and your chin out, and shoulder thrown back. Raise you right arm until it is level with your shoulder, pointing to the right. Turn your head and fix your gaze on your hand, and hold the arm perfectly steady for one minute. Repeat with the left arm. When you are able to perform this feat, perfectly, increase the time to two minutes, then to three, and so on until you are able to maintain the position for five minutes. The palm of the hand should be turned downward, this being the easiest position. By keeping the eyes fixed on the tips of the fingers; you will be able to see whether you are holding your arm perfectly steady.

3. Fill a wine glass full of water, and taking the glass between the fingers, extend the right arm directly in front of you. Fix the eyes upon the glass, and endeavor to hold the arm so steady that no quiver will be noticeable. Commence with one-minute exercises, and increase until the five-minute limit is reached. Alternate right and left arms.

4. In your everyday life, endeavor to avoid a tense, strained conditions of the muscles, when you should be at ease. Endeavor to acquire a

self-poised attitude and demeanor. Cultivate an easy, self-possessed manner, in preference to a nervous, strained, over-anxious appearance. Mental exercise will help you to acquire the proper carriage and demeanor. Stop beating the "devil's tattoo" on the table or chair. Such actions indicate a lack of self-control. Don't tap on the floor with your foot, nor swing your feet backward or forward while talking or sitting. Don't rock backward and forward in a rocking chair, as if you were working a machine at so much an hour. Don't bite your nails, nor chew your lips or cheek, don't wiggle your tongue around in your mouth, whilst reading or studying, or writing. Don't wink or blink your eyes. Get rid of any habit of twitching or jerking of any part of the body, which may have become second nature to you. You can stop it easily by "carrying the thought" and practicing concentering. Train yourself to bear with equanimity and composure, noises which have been startling you heretofore, such as the banging of a suddenly closed door, the dropping of a book or other object, etc. In other words, keep yourself well in hand. The above exercises will be of great assistance to you in getting yourself just where you want.

The above exercises were given to teach you the art of controlling involuntary muscular movement, thus bringing your body under the control of the voluntary functions. The following exercises are designed to enable you to bring you voluntary muscular movements under the direct control of the Will, in other words, to train the mental faculties producing voluntary muscular movement.

1. Sit in front of a table, placing your hands upon the table, the fists clinched and lying with the backs of the hands on the table, the thumb being doubled over the fingers. Fix your gaze upon the fist for a while, and then slowly extend. Then reverse the process, closing first the little finger and continuing the closing until the fist is again in its original position, with the thumb closed over the fingers. Repeat with the left hand. Continue this exercise five times at a sitting, and then increase it to ten times.

This exercise will make you "tired," but you must persevere as it is of importance to you in the directions of training your attention by directing it to trivial and monotonous exercises; in addition, it will give you direct control over all of your muscular movements. You soon will feel the benefit accruing from these simple and apparently unimportant exercises. Do not fail to keep the attention closely upon the closing and unclosing of the fingers. That is the main point, if you neglect it; you lose the entire benefit of the exercise.

2. This exercise is nothing more or less than the old trick, often observed among our country cousins, known as "twirling the thumbs." Place the fingers of one hand, leaving the thumbs free. Then slowly twirl the thumbs one over the other, with a circular motion. Be sure to keep the attention firmly fixed upon the ends of the thumbs.

3. Place the right hand on the knee, the fingers and thumb closed, with the exception of the first finger, which must be pointed out in front of you. Then move the finger slowly from side to side, keeping the attention firmly fixed upon the end of the finger.

These exercises may be extended indefinitely, and you may exercise your ingenuity in supplying additional one under this head. The main idea is that the exercise shall consist of some trivial, familiar, momentous muscular movement, and that the attention must be kept firmly fixed upon the moving part of the body. Your attention will revolt at the slavery enforced upon it, and will endeavor in every possible way to escape its thralldom. This is where the training comes in, and you must insist that your attention does its work, from beginning to end, and not wander away to more congenial scenes or occupations. Think of yourself as a strict schoolmaster, and of your attention as a playful, fun loving boy who tires of looking at his book and wishes to steal sly glances out of the window and door at the more attractive sights on the outside. Your business is to keep the boy at his book, knowing that it will be better for him, although he cannot see it just that way now. Before long, you will notice that you have much better control over your muscular movements, carriage and demeanor, and will also observe an increased power of attention and concentering in your everyday affairs, which will be of considerable advantage to you.

This class of exercises is intended to aid you in concentering your attention upon some material object not connected with yourself. Take some uninteresting object, such as a pencil, and concenter your entire attention upon it for five minutes. Look at it intently; everything of it; turn it over; consider it; think of its uses; its objects; of the materials of which it is made; the process of manufacturing, etc. Think of nothing else but the pencil. Imagine that your chief object in life is the study of that pencil. Imagine that there exists nothing else in the world but you and the pencil. "Only one world, and but two things in it, the pencil and I." Do not let your attention get away from the pencil, but keep it down to its work. You will realize what a rebellious creature your attention is when you try this exercise, but don't let him get the upper hand of you. It is very tiresome to him, but it is for his own good, so stick to it. When you have conquered the rebellious attention you will have achieved a greater victory that you now realize. Many a time in after life, when you need the closest attention upon some matter before you, you will thank me for "putting you on" to this exercise.

This exercise can be varied each day, always choosing some uninteresting and familiar object upon which to concenter the attention. Don't select an interesting object; for it requires no effort to concenter upon that. You need something that will seem like "work" to the attention. The less interesting the object—the more the work—and the better the exercise. The trouble with this exercise is, that you will soon run out of material, as the continued concentering of the attention upon uninteresting objects will, in the end, cause the attention, in self defense, to take an interest in the things upon which it concenters. However, when you have reached this stage, you will have but little further need of the exercise, as you then will be able to concenter your attention upon anything, or anybody.

The above exercises will be sufficient for your purpose, it being understood that you will extend the several exercises by material supplied by your own invention and ingenuity. You may practice upon something occurring in your everyday world. You will not be at a loss for material upon which to practice, now that you have the main idea impressed upon you memory.

The exercises given in the preceding lessons can be practiced more intelligently, now that you understand the advantage to be gained by concentering. You will be able to "carry the thought" better, to direct more energy into suggestions, and into the projection of thought vibrations. Your eye exercises will take on a new phase, and so will the exercises in Telepathic Volation, etc. You will be able to overcome bad habits, and acquire good habits in their place. In short, by the acquirement of the art of concentering, you will be able to do everything better than formerly. You will have acquired a firm control over body and mind, and will find that you are now the master of your inclinations, not their slave. The power gained over yourself will manifest itself in the power to control others. The man, who conquers himself, has no trouble in impressing his will upon others. Continue the practice of concentering and developing the amenability of the Mind to the Will, and you will become a giant, compared to men who have not acquired this power. Try your will power on yourself in different ways, until you feel confident that you have won the mastery of self. Be satisfied with nothing else. When you have gained that, the mastery of others is already yours.

Chapter 15

VALEDICTORY

Intuitive perception of the truth—A mere hint at a great truth—Latent powers developed—The practical side—The occult side—An understanding of the Science of the Mind has an elevating effect—Recognition of the Ego—A literature of froth and bubbles—A few grains of wheat among the chaff—Practical knowledge scarce, but demanded—Advice to seekers after the truth—The small flame within you—A three-fold mighty dynamic force—"I AM" strength—New resolves, new strength—The Brotherhood of Man—Self-respect—Do not be imposed upon—Don't be a yellow dog— A short rule of action—Do not misuse your new found power—A hint at a great truth— Farewell advice

I feel that those who have followed me through the preceding lessons must have felt within them the intuitive assurance of the Truth contained in the instruction herein given. In a work of this size and character, I can do no more that merely direct the Mind; to give them a hint of the great Truth; to acquaint them with a few exercises which, if followed conscientiously, will enable them to develop their latent powers. More than this would be beyond the scope of this work, which is intended to give popular instruction in the exercise and use of Personal Magnetism and Psychic Influence in the affairs of everyday life. The average reader will rest satisfied with the "practical" side of the subject, and will not feel inclined to enter into the occult phase. To the few who feel an inclination to pursue the subject still further, who would penetrate behind the veil, there are other sources of information open, which I will be pleased to point out to those who may so request. A letter will reach me if address to me at 30 Auditorium Building, Chicago.

Without attempting to go further into the subject, I would say that in my opinion, an intelligent understanding of the laws underlying the Science of Mind, supplies one with a most elevating rule of life and conduct; brings to man a realizing sense of his own individuality, strength and power—a consciousness of the reality and immanence of his real self, the I AM. The recognition of the Ego carries with it a sense of new duties and the means of performing them.

The student of what is known as the "New Thought" finds himself surrounded with a mass of literature, much of which consists of froth and bubbles. Grains of thought are there, but are surrounded by bushels of verbal chaff. The searcher for ideas receives—words, words, and words. The works on the subject, which are really worth the time and trouble of reading, are few, and the student, alas, knows not where to find them Practical. Understandable works on this subject are being demanded by many minds and following the invariable rule, which causes the production of the thing which is earnestly demanded, works of this kind are sure to appear. Speed the day.

To the student I would say, do not be deluded by "isms" or leaders; you possess within you the real Truth, and it will manifest itself to you, in time developing gradually and naturally, as the flower. The recognition of the I AM will bring its reward. The small flame within will throw light on all subjects and illuminate them.

Pursue your way through life, earnestly and calmly. Hurry is not Hast; Bustle is not Energy; Noise is not Strength. The man of quiet calm, earnest and persistent qualities reaches the goal long before his brother of opposite tendencies. Confidence, Expectation and Calm Demand is a three-fold, mighty dynamic force, which would solve many problems if man but realized it. The wise man uses that which the fool neglects. "The stone which the builders rejected becomes the cornerstone of the temple."

Do not crawl on your belly, like a worm; do not humble yourself in the dust and call upon heaven to witness what a despicable creature you are; do not call yourself a "miserable sinner," worthy only of eternal damnation. No! A thousand times, No! Rise to your feet; raise your head and face the skies; throw back your shoulders, and fill your lungs with Nature's ozone. Then say to yourself,

I AM a part of the Eternal Life Principle:
I AM created after the Divine image;
I AM filled with Divine Breath of Life;
Nothing can hurt ME,
For I AM a part of the Eternal.

Go your way, friend, strong in your new resolves, strong in your new-found strength. Do your duty, first to yourself; then to your fellowmen. Recognize the Brotherhood of Man; realize that all men are your brothers—pretty poor lot of relations, but brothers at that. Do not impose on your brother-man, but do not let him impose on you. If you give in to him against your judgment and conscience, you not only hurt yourself, but also injure him. Do not start fights; but let no man smite you with impunity. If a man smites you on one cheek, do not turn to him the other, but do a little smiting on your own account—and smite hard. Do not smite him with Hate in your heart, and do not hesitate to forgive him after he has "come to." The doctrine of nonresistance is misunderstood; it does not mean that you should be a backboneless creature—a sheep-like, rabbit-hearted specimen of humanity. No, no; when you allow a man to impose on you and wrong you, you are not acting right toward the other man; duty to him demands that you let him know just "where he is at." I am speaking of real aggression or invasion of your rights, now, not of fancied wrongs or mountains made of mole-hills; that is the other extreme. But do not allow Hate to find a lodging place in your heart. Go through the world "with the grace of God in your heart, and a good, strong hickory club in your hand." Don't use the club for offense (never do that), but keep it around to defend yourself with. If you are "clad in the armor of a righteous cause," and the world sees that you have self-respect and will stand no nonsense, it will treat you with respect. The dog who maintains a confident, calm demeanor, is in but little danger of feeling the boot-toe of the passerby but the white-livered cur who draws himself up, and places his tail between his legs that he may present a better aim for the kick—gets the kick. He gets what he expects. What is true of the dog is equally true of the man. If you have followed the advice and instructions contained in this little work, you will not have many kicks aimed at you. But, remember—no kicking of dogs on your part—you must be above that.

An old writer has summed up mans duty to man in the following words, which should be inscribed in letters of gold over every doorway in the land:

"Wrong no man, and render unto every man his due."

If the above words form the rule of action, and life, of men, there would be no need of lawyers, courts, or prisons; life would then seem "one long, sweet song." Try to do your part in bringing about this result. Once more, I caution you not to misuse your newfound power, do not drag the gift of the Spirit through the mud.

Use it freely, in your own behalf, in every legitimate way, but harm no man by reason of, or by means of it. If you fail to grasp the meaning of any of the teachings contained in this little work, do not feel discouraged, for it will come to you later. Read over the lessons, which seem to be most difficult to you, and then place yourself in the relaxed condition of body, and mind. *Enter the silence*—and a new light will break upon you.

"Knock and it shall be opened unto you; ask and ye shall receive."

And now, friends, we have come to the parting of the ways. We may meet again, but, if not, let us part feeling that we are none the worse for the short acquaintance. If I have done you any good, if I have awakened in you new thoughts, hopes and aspirations, may you make them manifest in actions and results.

Our little journey, along the banks of the stream, has been pleasant to me, and I trust that I have not bored you, nor caused you to regret the acquaintance—not a chance acquaintance, you may rest assured, for "nothing ever happens."

www.ingramcontent.com/pod-product-compliance
Lightning Source LLC
Chambersburg PA
CBHW022124280326
41933CB00007B/533